Unabashedly Episcopalian

Unabashedly Episcopalian

Proclaiming the Good News
of the Episcopal Church

C. ANDREW DOYLE

Morehouse Publishing
NEW YORK · HARRISBURG · DENVER

Morehouse Publishing, 4775 Linglestown Road, Harrisburg, PA 17112

Morehouse Publishing, 445 Fifth Avenue, New York, NY 10016

Morehouse Publishing is an imprint of Church Publishing Incorporated. www.churchpublishing.org

Cover design by Laurie Klein Westhafer
Typeset by Vicki K. Black

Library of Congress Cataloging-in-Publication Data

Doyle, C. Andrew.
  Unabashedly Episcopalian : proclaiming the good news of the Episcopal church / C. Andrew Doyle.
      p.   cm.
  Includes bibliographical references.
  ISBN 978-0-8192-2808-6 (pbk.) -- ISBN 978-0-8192-2809-3 (ebook) 1. Episcopal Church. I. Title.
  BX5930.3.D69 2012
  283'.73--dc23
                                        2012021419

Printed in the United States of America

Contents

What is the good news of the Episcopal Church?

The good news is that in our Episcopal Church
we love God in Christ Jesus,
we love our tradition,
and we love our relationships.

Acknowledgments

This book is envisioned to help some who pick it up to hear our unique witness of God through the tradition of the Episcopal Church. For still others this book is an opportunity to see our church again for the first time. I love Jesus and I love our tradition. I am unabashedly Episcopalian and want others to experience the love of God and our church as I have experienced them over these many years.

I am grateful to JoAnne, my wife, who encouraged me to write. I am very thankful for the Reverend Kelly Demo, who helped me get started by collecting my written texts from various sermons and talks into something I could work with. I also am thankful for the Reverend Stephanie Spellers, my editor at Church Publishing, who cheered me on to the completion of the work and offered a labor of love through the final edits.

Most of all, though, I am grateful for the long line of Doyles and Illingworths who passed their tradition to my loving parents Charles and Sylvia Ann, who in turn gave me the opportunity to see the spiritual depth, wisdom, and tradition of our Episcopal Church. They taught me to pray. My dad was an Episcopal priest and he instilled in me a love for our worship and history. Both my parents also believed the beauty of the liturgy was itself connected and intertwined with works which made people's lives better. Growing up during the Civil Rights era and Vietnam War, they inspired a commitment to bearing a gospel witness to the world come where it will, and cost what it may.

For all these and many countless blessings I have received from the Episcopal Church, I am thankful.

> Almighty God, Father of all mercies, we your unworthy servants give you humble thanks for all your goodness and loving-kindness to us and to all whom you have made. We bless you for our creation, preservation, and all the blessings of this life; but above all for your immeasurable love in the redemption of the world by our Lord Jesus Christ; for the means of grace, and for the hope of glory. And, we pray, give us such an awareness of your mercies, that with truly thankful hearts we may show forth your praise, not only with our lips, but in our lives, by giving up our selves to your service, and by walking before you in holiness and righteousness all our days; through Jesus Christ our Lord, to whom, with you and the Holy Spirit, be honor and glory throughout all ages. Amen.[1]

chapter one

We Are Episcopalian

We are tied together in a single garment
of destiny, caught in an inescapable
network of mutuality.

— THE REV. DR. MARTIN LUTHER KING, JR.

n Wednesday, September 7, 1774, at the inau-
gural session of the Continental Congress, with
the weight of war and the hope of freedom on
their minds, the Reverend Jacob Duché, an Anglican
clergyman and rector of Christ Church in Philadelphia,
was invited to read prayers to the Congress. As it hap-
pened, the 35th Psalm was appointed in the *Book of
Common Prayer* as a part of Morning Prayer that day.
Duché began, "Plead my cause, O Lord, with them that
strive with me: fight against them that fight against me.
Take hold of shield and buckler, and stand up for mine
help."[2]

On June 28, 1836, it was an Episcopal service that
accompanied James Madison, our fourth president and
founding father, to his grave.[3] And they were Episcopal
prayers that comforted the mourners in their grief.

It was an Episcopal service of Morning Prayer with
hymns that inaugurated the Atlantic Charter between
British Prime Minister Winston Churchill and American
President Franklin D. Roosevelt on the deck of the
HMS *Prince of Wales* on the eve of World War II.[4] And
at the service commemorating Roosevelt's third inauguration, in the midst of war, an Episcopal prayer was
used to petition for our enemies and pray for peace.[5]

As an Episcopal seminarian, Jonathan M. Daniels
followed the call of Martin Luther King, Jr. to come to
Selma, Alabama, where he lived with an African-American family and helped integrate the local Episcopal
Church. On August 20, 1965, Daniels was shot while
saving the life of a young black woman.

Three years later, at the Washington National Cathedral (an Episcopal church), Dr. Martin Luther King, Jr.
climbed the thirteen steps into the pulpit during an Episcopal service and said:

We are tied together in the single garment of destiny, caught in an inescapable network of mutuality. And whatever affects one directly affects all indirectly. For some strange reason, I can never be what I ought to be until you are what you ought to be. And you can never be what you ought to be until I am what I ought to be. This is the way God's universe is made; this is the way it is structured.[6]

I remember watching on television then president-elect Barack Obama begin his day by walking into St. John's Episcopal Church, Lafayette Square, prior to being sworn in as our 44th president of the United States on January 20, 2009. In the days surrounding the inauguration he would attend a national prayer service in Washington National Cathedral, and deliver a speech on the steps of the Lincoln Memorial where Martin Luther King, Jr. dreamed his dream.

In New York City, on September 11, 2001, St. Paul's Chapel (the chapel in which George Washington, our first president, worshiped following his inauguration) became an epicenter for relief workers and a nation in crisis. In this modest chapel of the venerable Trinity Episcopal Church, Wall Street, some five thousand volunteers transformed an eighteenth-century landmark into a sacramental vessel pouring out love and care.

Episcopal relief workers have rebuilt homes, assembled temporary shelters, and provided clean drinking water in the wake of tsunamis, earthquakes, and hurricanes. After Hurricane Katrina we led efforts to rebuild cities across the Gulf Coast from Mississippi to New Orleans to Texas. We have housed tens of thousands in Haiti. We have labored in the midst of the urban poor and bleak rural desolation.

The Episcopal Church welcomes all and we have a tradition of putting into action the words of Isaiah, which Jesus spoke in the synagogue in Nazareth (Luke 4:18–19): "The Spirit of the Lord is upon me, because he has anointed me to bring good news to the poor. He has sent me to proclaim release to the captives and recovery of sight to the blind, to let the oppressed go free, to proclaim the year of the Lord's favor." Like Jesus himself, we the faithful members of the Episcopal Church have sought through the years to make God's love incarnational—to make God's love real in the mission and ministry of our church.

The Episcopal Church is the community in which I was raised, the son of a priest. It is the faith tradition that I was baptized into at the college chapel on the campus of Southern Methodist University, where my parents helped to lead the Episcopal Student Center. It is the tradition I studied as a young adult prior to my own confirmation; having memorized the Lord's Prayer, the Nicene Creed, and the Catechism (or the church's teachings) from the back of the "new" *Book of Common Prayer* of 1979. I knelt before Bishop Jose Guadalupe Saucedo of Mexico, at that time a diocese of the Episcopal Church, and was confirmed. I came to appreciate this tradition even more in my adult years as a summer camp counselor and camp staff member at Camp Allen, an Episcopal camp northwest of Houston, as a participant in college mission at the Canterbury Association at the University of North Texas, and as a member of the staff at St. Stephen's Episcopal School in Austin, Texas.

When I discerned a call to serve Jesus Christ in the ordained ministry, the Episcopal Church gave voice to my own faith and belief in God and God's revelation.

The tradition of daily Morning Prayer and the singing of hymns and canticles rang throughout my theological studies at Virginia Theological Seminary. The words and prayers of the *Book of Common Prayer* comforted me as I ministered to the victims and their families at a deadly bonfire collapse at Texas A&M University in 1999.

This tradition has supported me at my best and challenged me at my worst. In this church, I have found the clearest reflection I know of the one, holy, catholic, and apostolic faith delivered to the saints and handed down through generations of the faithful. This faith sung and prayed by a thousand tongues before me—this is the church I love. It is the Episcopal Church and its particular and unique witness to Jesus Christ that inspires me to mission and inspires my desire to be a better bishop and human being.

Bound by a Promise

Why begin a book geared to the newly baptized and confirmed, and those who long to recall those vows, in this fashion? You have taken a profound oath to God and to your community in the sacrament of baptism and/or confirmation or by reception into the Anglican Communion, and you have done it specifically in the context of an Episcopal Church. You have made a covenant with God, one that is rooted in the waters of baptism.

It is my hope that, as you turn these pages, you will explore your sacred promises to God and walk your pilgrim journey with greater intention. More importantly, I hope you will find what many have found: that God is calling you to serve and minister in the world around you. The combined work of prayer and mission has been the bedrock of the Episcopal Church (and the larger Anglican Communion) since its birth in the sixteenth century and its development under the leadership of Queen Elizabeth I and the Stuart kings in the 1600s. You are a part of a long line of Anglicans who— strengthened by liturgy, sacrament, prayer, and Scripture—take their faith seriously.

In the Episcopal Church we understand that our promises are to God *and* to our fellow human beings as well. These are promises made to help build up stone by stone the reign of God, and they are promises made for the communities in which we live and move and have our being, the communities we call home.

The reality is that the Episcopal Church has always found its mission rooted in contexts across our country and across the sixteen other nations worldwide in which we find our home.[7] We are a great and global church with wide-reaching partnerships that are changing lives on a daily basis. Countless people whose names we know and even more whose names we do not know have called on the strength of our tradition and our liturgies, from the firefighter at Ground Zero to the woman in the pew praying the Psalms out of the Prayer Book.

It is my prayer that you, in your own life, will find that same strength. It is my hope that all who are seeking might find in the Episcopal Church the possibility and reality of a strong relationship with God. I pray that you will find a store of wisdom you can draw on when you are unsure of a course of action. May you find a deep well of spirituality that you can draw from when you are in trouble, fearful, or in pain, as well as when you are celebrating life's joys. I hope you will discover that the firm foundation of Jesus Christ revealed in our baptismal promises and in our tradition will be a foundation upon which you may, with others, reshape the world. We in the Episcopal Church have a particular and beautiful way of understanding the redeeming work of Jesus Christ, and we stand as bearers of the gift of God's abundant grace for humankind.

There will come a time in your life, a moment when every word will matter, every prayer spoken or silently prayed will count, every action will be an opportunity for change. Into these moments, let the wisdom of our Episcopal heritage, worship, prayer, and Scripture be present for you, uphold you, and sustain you.

We do all of this worship and prayer and tenacious pursuit of living out our faith for one reason. We are called through Christ's own love and by our baptism to devote our lives to the coming of the reign of God. We understand a virtuous citizenship that beckons us to fulfill our duty and responsibility as missionaries of God's love in the world around us. So we pray:

> Send us now into the world in peace,
> and grant us strength and courage
> to love and serve you
> with gladness and singleness of heart;
> through Jesus Christ our Lord. Amen.[8]

chapter two

Choosing to Walk the Pilgrim Way

Celebrant   Do you desire to be baptized?

Candidate   I do.[9]

Jesus said, "Follow me."

— LUKE 9:23

Sociologists, observers of culture, and church leaders have been talking for some time about an important book: *Soul Searching: The Religious and Spiritual Lives of American Teenagers*. Published in 2005, the book is based upon some three thousand interviews with teenagers, and it highlights the emerging sensibilities of this new generation of spiritual pilgrims.

The authors claim that five concepts make up the foundation of this generation's faith, which together add up to a perspective they call *moralistic therapeutic deism*. It asserts the following beliefs:

1. A God exists who created and orders the world and watches over human life on earth.
2. God wants people to be good, nice, and fair to each other, as taught in the Bible and by most world religions.
3. The central goal of life is to be happy and to feel good about oneself.
4. God does not need to be particularly involved in one's life except when God is needed to resolve a problem.
5. Good people go to heaven when they die.[10]

This is not a bad set of beliefs to live by. In fact if the whole world abided by these basic beliefs it would be a far better place. But I would say that we as Episcopalians have a different way of seeing the world and our place in it. When we are asked if we wish to be baptized, or when we reaffirm our baptism, we step forward and say to the world that we believe differently. There are some things we hold in common with all religious beliefs and others we hold in common with the larger family of Christian believers. But when we rise and affirm the faith of the church and reaffirm our own faith, we are challenged to be a particular and unique people of God.

Not Just Any God

The Baptismal Covenant we make with God and our communities says we believe in a God who created and ordered the world *but* who ordered it for a particular purpose: for beauty and relationship. We believe in a God who watches over human life *and* interacts with all life on earth, with a particular relationship to the human community, through Jesus Christ. We have faith in a God who desires that people be good, nice, and fair to each other, and who says we have a responsibility to take care of each other when we are poor, hungry, alone or in need.

We accept as true that Jesus Christ is the living, resurrected example of how humanity is to treat one another, and that we ought to seek to emulate his Way. While it is a good thing to be happy and to feel good about oneself, we do not believe that this is the *central goal* in life. Our faith teaches us that God asks us to sacrifice our lives for others' sakes.

The center of our life is God, and God most identifies with the weak and poor. We believe focusing on consumerism creates disordered lives that are out of proportion with the wider needs of the world around us. We believe in a God who is with us in our problems and with us when things are going well. We believe in a God who is a companion along the way (Luke 24), who calls us "friends" (John 15:15), and who eats and drinks with sinners (Mark 2:16). The God we proclaim is present with us in all our doings. We do believe in the kingdom of heaven, but we believe that we participate in bringing it to life today. We do not spend a lot of time concerned with life after death; we spend most of our time working to make heaven real in this world. We remind ourselves that Jesus' work was teaching and proclaiming the good news of the kingdom of God and curing every disease and every sickness among the people, and that he said, "Follow me" (Luke 9:1–23).

When we as Episcopalians step forward and choose to make our confession of faith, we remove ourselves from a general belief in a general God who participates generally in our life. We choose specifically to walk the pilgrim way with God and to live out a particular revelation found uniquely in the Episcopal Church.

Not Just Any People

Geneticists speak of something called a *meme*. The concept originated with Richard Dawkins, a geneticist who has also gained fame as part of the atheist dialogues that are currently popular. Meme theory is basically the application of Darwinian genetic theory to culture, language, and narrative. Dawkins argues that the human attachment to God comes out of fear and anxiety about having our basic needs met. For Dawkins God is like a story—or a genetic trait or a meme—that keeps getting replicated because of our anxiety and fear.

As you can imagine, Dawkins and I disagree. For the Christian, words have meaning and substance. What we say is very real. But that language is more than a social construct. As people of the Word of God, we believe our language and our actions are rooted in the language and activity of God. We believe that what was spoken before all that is seen and unseen is the ground of our proclamation today. When we stand up and make our promises before God with the congregation and community as our witness, we create a verbal vessel of grace that makes its way through creation and draws us ever closer to the divine being and to one another.

You and I are making in our faith statements not simply promises about how we believe; we are also making statements about the kind of people we wish to become, and the type of world we wish to live in. When we step forward, we are saying we are not atheists or even just good people. When we step forward, we are proclaiming that we are Episcopalians and that we have a particular and unique vision of the world around us.

This unique worldview is not formed by capitalism or some political theory. Our Episcopal worldview is formed through a life lived in connection with sacraments.

In the Episcopal Church there are two gospel sacraments: one is the Eucharist and one is baptism. These are considered to be gospel sacraments because Jesus gives them to humanity and the church as specific signs of the grace of God. We say we have seven sacraments (like the Roman Church) and we do; but for Anglicans the five additional sacraments are secondary and are not given by Jesus Christ to the church. Instead, the sacraments of confirmation (the second half of baptism), marriage, anointing the sick, reconciliation, and ordination are fondly referred to as sacraments with a little "s" because it is the church itself which believes they are sacramental vessels of God's grace. They are not necessary in the life lived to God, though they can aid in a life lived with God. In the words of our catechism, we believe all of the sacraments are "outward and visible signs of inward and spiritual grace, given by Christ as sure and certain means by which we receive that grace."[11]

Not Just Any Church

When we step forward and make our promises as baptized Episcopalians, we say we believe in a particular kind of church. No other church globally (except those who began as missionary churches of the Episcopal Church) has a Baptismal Covenant quite like ours.[12]

By answering the questions at the heart of the Baptismal Covenant, beginning with the question asked in the presentation, "Do you desire to be baptized?" we are stepping into a church that is a particular community grounded in the ministry of Jesus Christ, whose ministry was a continuation of the Torah life of our Jewish faith ancestors.

We are also proclaiming our faith as part of living today, physically putting on the church we claim as our own. We are becoming Episcopalians. We are choosing, as I think you will discover, a particular rule of life. Not unlike the communities in which the authors wrote the gospels of Matthew, Mark, Luke, or John, we today make our communal life particular in our place and time. We are unique and rooted in our contemporary contexts, and yet connected to our ancestors.

We understand that an important part of being the church is returning to the Bible. There are many pop movements and psychological and philosophical treatises out in the world, but we proclaim uniquely that we will live by the rule found in a certain body of work which stretches out over generations and which we call the Holy Scriptures. The church is described in these texts as a body of which Christ is the head and of which all baptized persons are members. Saint Paul wrote, "And God has put all things under his feet and has made him the head over all things for the church, which is his body, the fullness of him who fills all in all" (Ephesians 1:22).

The Baptismal Covenant begins with an affirmation of the Apostles' Creed. In the creed, the church is described as one, holy, catholic, and apostolic. This proclamation of unity is a challenging one. If it were dependent on our actions, that unity would be a pipedream. It is not. The church is constantly enacting in great and small measures the unified body—the incarnational body—of Jesus Christ in the world. That is an action of God, not of human undertaking. Now, humans can certainly damage and even break it, but that does not make the church as an expression of God's life in the world any less real. No one steps forward for baptism or confirmation without the congregation promising to support them in their life in Christ as a member of the Episcopal Church and body of Christ; and no one ever makes covenantal promises to God alone. In this we see an expression of the unity of the church.

The questions every disciple must ask are, "Am I living into this unity or not? Am I consciously seeking to be a part of that one church, or seeking my own way?"

When we present someone to be baptized—child or adult—the vision is not only of individual transformation but of an always evolving body of Christ. Episcopalians believe, as did the ancient Christians, that when you are baptized you are being initiated into the body of Christ. We believe that what is being made visible in baptism is the unity and grace that is part of the community of the faithful church at worship and at work in the world.

We Will, With God's Help

Now, we come to the question of what we desire: "Do you desire to be baptized?" The person says yes, or family members say yes on behalf of the child who will be confirmed later. Baptism and confirmation are two parts of the same service. They really are not two separate services, but when the church grew to the extent that bishops were no longer present in every congregation and baptisms were done by the priests, they divided the service so that the anointing and laying on of hands by the bishop would take place later, when the bishop came to visit. Either way, the service begins by getting clarity that you desire this sacramental life or that people who love you are offering it to you.

Then we arrive at another set of questions: The Renunciations.

Do you renounce Satan and all the spiritual forces
of wickedness that rebel against God?

Do you renounce the evil powers of this world
which corrupt and destroy the creatures of God?

Do you renounce all sinful desires that draw you
from the love of God?

Do you turn to Jesus Christ and accept him as
your Savior?

Do you put your whole trust in his grace and love?

Do you promise to follow and obey him as your
Lord?

You cannot get to the Baptismal Covenant without first
answering these questions. We do not get to our defini-
tion of God or our promises to read Scripture and participate in worship, to strive for justice and peace and
the dignity of every human being, without considering
these commitments and establishing this foundation.

From there, we continue to build with the Baptismal
Covenant, which begins with an affirmation of our faith
in the Trinitarian God, in the form of question and re-
sponses based on the Apostles' Creed.

Celebrant	Do you believe in God the Father?
People	I believe in God, the Father almighty, creator of heaven and earth.
Celebrant	Do you believe in Jesus Christ, the Son of God?
People	I believe in Jesus Christ, his only Son, our Lord. He was conceived by the power of the Holy Spirit and born of the Virgin Mary. He suffered under

Pontius Pilate, was crucified, died, and was buried. He descended to the dead. On the third day he rose again. He ascended into heaven, and is seated at the right hand of the Father. He will come again to judge the living and the dead.

Celebrant   Do you believe in God the Holy Spirit?

People   I believe in the Holy Spirit, the holy catholic Church, the communion of saints, the forgiveness of sins, the resurrection of the body, and the life everlasting.

The covenant continues from that general statement of faith, a faith we share with Christians the world over, to name the uniqueness of the Episcopal way of following Jesus. These five promises serve as the heart of the Baptismal Covenant.

Celebrant   Will you continue in the apostles' teaching and fellowship, in the breaking of bread, and in the prayers?

People   I will, with God's help.

Celebrant   Will you persevere in resisting evil, and, whenever you fall into sin, repent and return to the Lord?

People   I will, with God's help.

Celebrant   Will you proclaim by word and example the Good News of God in Christ?

People   I will, with God's help.

Celebrant	Will you seek and serve Christ in all persons, loving your neighbor as yourself?
People	I will, with God's help.
Celebrant	Will you strive for justice and peace among all people, and respect the dignity of every human being?
People	I will, with God's help.

You can see that we believe in a particular God, who is creator and savior of a particular world in which we are helping to bring about a particular kingdom in a particular way. We are taking on a discipline as a Christian, and I would say uniquely as an Episcopalian, and we should not mistakenly assume everybody makes these promises in baptism.

Every denominational framework is unique. This one is ours. When I talk about being unabashedly Episcopalian, I am promising to act and speak out against spiritual forces that rebel against God and the story of God and our understanding of who God is and the world that God created. With clarity, we are saying we will act and speak out against powers which corrupt God's creation, which move creation from sustainability to a mere commodity for consumption, corrupting and destroying the creatures of God. We are expressing a personal willingness to bring intention to those daily choices that place us closer or further from the will of God in Jesus Christ. We are going to aim toward Jesus as the highest form of a life lived in God's community, and we are going to trust that God's love and grace will enable us to do this work.

As a bishop, every week I have the incredible honor to stand with those making a confession of faith. I have the privilege of walking with communities as they say yes to the promises of God. Week after week I have the opportunity to remake, rethink, remind, and begin again to remold my own life. I constantly have before me these questions: How am I doing as a Christian and as an Episcopalian? How am I doing in my life and these promises day after day after day?

When we step forward, we step forward together. When we speak our *yes* to God's invitation, we speak with one voice. As Episcopalians we, together, make a conscious decision to live within the walls of the kingdom of God.

I am reminded of the words and witness of the poet and Anglican priest R. S. Thomas. In his poem entitled "The Kingdom" he writes:

> It's a long way off but inside it
> There are quite different things going on:
> ...admission
> Is free, if you purge yourself
> Of desire, and present yourself with
> Your need only and the simple offering
> Of your faith, green as a leaf.[13]

We present ourselves and choose together to make our pilgrim way in this world. We choose God's unexpected, upside-down kingdom over all others. That is how our journey begins.

chapter three

Telling the One, True Story

Celebrant	Do you believe in God the Father?
Candidate	I believe in God, the Father almighty, creator of heaven and earth.[14]

Make a joyful noise to the Lord, all the earth.
Worship the Lord with gladness;
    come into his presence with singing.
Know that the Lord is God.
It is he that made us, and we are his;
    we are his people,
    and the sheep of his pasture.
Enter his gates with thanksgiving,
    and his courts with praise.
Give thanks to him, bless his name.
For the Lord is good;
    his steadfast love endures forever,
    and his faithfulness to all generations.

— PSALM 100

𝕴 have two daughters, and as they were growing up we read a story to them every night. Sometimes it was a short story or a picture book, and other times we delved into chapter books. Still, since the very beginning, for 3,982 nights, we have read them stories. And these 3,982 nights (give or take a few), I have waited patiently.

I remember in my mind's eye that they would scurry to me, their blond ringlets in scarlet ribbons, looking up at me with big angelic eyes and pleading, "Father, Father dearest" (remember, this is a dream), "would you read to us *The Day that Fletcher Hatched*?"

"Yes, my darling children," I say, with a sigh. We read their choice and I send them off to bed.

The next night comes, and the next. I keep hoping they will ask me to tell them this one story, the story I have come to know by heart. One night, I hit the limit and blurt out: "But, don't you want to hear The Story, the story of the people of Israel?"

"Dad!" (Cue eye roll.) "We want Captain Underpants!" So I give in.

But if on one of these nights (they continue even now with my younger daughter—Harry Potter naturally), if they were to say, "Yes, yes, Father, tell us The Story," I would pause in my most prayerful and mindful manner, perhaps putting my hands to my lips in a prayerful position. And I would begin, "O Best Beloved, the Lord is good, and his mercy is everlasting. And in a high and far off place, somewhere outside of Egypt on the third day, on the third new moon after the Israelites had gone out of the land of Egypt into the wilderness, our good Lord told his people some very important things. He said to them, 'I will bear you up on eagle's wings, and I will bring you to myself. You will be my treasured possession for you are my people, and you will be holy, and you will be a kingdom of priests.' That, O Best Beloved, is what God told his people because God is good, and his mercy is everlasting." I would share with them this, the one, true story.

I think it is as primal a need to tell and hear stories like this as it is to eat and sleep. Certainly we as humans have been blessed to hear the stories of our ancestors. We seek our own personal stories, as well: the stories of our parents and the stories of our origins. Perhaps it is an American thing (a young country's nature) to long to hear the stories of our founding and to know where we have come from.

In the South it is the first thing people do when they meet one another. They ask questions and give permission for others to tell their stories. Then they try to figure out how they are related or how their relatives and friends might know one another. Our stories tell us who we are as individuals, but our stories also tell us who we are as a community.

The Church's Story

Storytelling forms us as individuals, as families, and as communities, and it forms who we are as a church. The Episcopal Church has a story. We tell stories every single Sunday. Our liturgy is woven with the stories of our faith ancestors. We retell the stories in hymns and by reading Scripture. We listen to the faithful journeys and lives of ancestors like Abraham and Sarah, Isaac and Rebekah, Jacob and Rachel. We retell the stories of

David and Solomon and all those who ruled Israel. We tell the story of the prophets. We read our faith ancestors' prayers. We listen and recount their dreams and prophecies.

In our liturgy we tell the story of Jesus, his life, mission, and ministry, and his death and resurrection. We read the letters of the earliest communities. We tell our sacred story as we recount the story of those who followed Jesus.

Ultimately every person you meet, whether they realize it or not, needs to hear the words, "O Beloved One, the Lord is good. His mercy is everlasting. The Lord bears you up on eagle's wings and draws you near because you are a treasure to our God and you are his possession and you are to be holy and you are a member of an eternal priesthood." As I said, people may not even realize their heart wants to hear that story. But surely they do.

In fact, I have known people who cannot believe they are beloved, by another person or even by God. Some will work very hard not to tell or listen to the story, and that is understandable because it is very powerful. This story unmoors our individual anchoring as the center of the universe, proclaiming that we are not alone and we are not all powerful and we are not all knowing. It holds us accountable for our actions and challenges us to see people as God created them, precious in God's eyes.

The Episcopal Church proclaims a gospel story week after week that reminds people they are the beloved of God. The Episcopal Church also proclaims a gospel that reminds us that we are to seek to feed the hungry, clothe the naked, and meet the needs of those of us who are poor. Whenever we gather, we are reminded that God has created us as a diverse, multi-ethnic people, and that we are beautiful and different. That is the case now, and it has been the case among God's people since the beginning.

You have the ability to step into your church and into wilderness places beyond the church to tell people that—though they may think they see death—there is life. The Episcopal Church believes in a God who calls us beloved, and, because of that faith, we see possibilities where there are dead ends. You carry within you the ability to announce to all the people in your life— in your office, in your school, in your home—that God loves even in the midst of hate, that God offers redemption where there is imprisonment and reconciliation where there is brokenness. The Lord is good, and his mercy is everlasting.

God Is With Us

Our church has existed over the years as part of the great lineage of Western Christianity. Our church believes in a God who was present before the beginning of creation. We believe in a God who created out of God's own desire, who longs to walk with his creation in the garden of his own making in the cool of the day (Genesis 3:8). God looks upon all of creation and sees beauty and holiness reflected back into the heavens.

Our God has been present through the building up and the tearing down of whole civilizations. Perhaps most miraculously, God's presence is everywhere and with everyone: with the young and the old, the poor and the rich, the sinner and the righteous, with those who are far off and with those who are near, in life and death, war and peace, in division of the church itself and in the sweetness of communion. God has ensured that no one comes into this world alone or enters the greater life of saints alone. This God we believe in is faithful and would never abandon us.

O Best Beloved, in the midst of our trials, God bears us up on eagle's wings, and brings us to himself. God is good, and his mercy is everlasting.

The God I bear witness to in my ministry as a bishop in the Episcopal Church is a God who is present in homeless shelters, rehab programs, schools, hospitals, and churches, on the streets, in coffee shops, and in people's homes. God is present with us today in all God's beauty and holiness, and I have the incredible pleasure to see God's people at work pointing out to countless others how God is molding and shaping, caring and loving, holding fast and letting go.

The God we proclaim has been with us in the midst of our communities and has always beckoned us to join him in the world, walking in the eve of the day. The members of the Episcopal Church have believed that it was their responsibility to walk with God in faith in the world. This is what it really means to be a saint. Saints are those who by their lives bear witness to God, whose mercy and kindness and gentleness is everlasting.

We Episcopalians are fond of a hymn we often sing in November, around All Saints' Day, as we remember the countless lives of those witnesses who have come before us. The words are these:

> I sing a song of the saints of God,
> patient and brave and true,

who toiled and fought and lived and died
for the Lord they loved and knew.
And one was a doctor, and one was a queen,
and one was a shepherdess on the green:
they were all of them saints of God—and I mean,
God helping, to be one too.

They loved their Lord so dear, so dear,
and his love made them strong;
and they followed the right, for Jesus' sake,
the whole of their good lives long.
And one was a soldier, and one was a priest,
and one was slain by a fierce wild beast:
and there's not any reason—no, not the least,
why I shouldn't be one too.

They lived not only in ages past,
there are hundreds of thousands still,
the world is bright with the joyous saints
who love to do Jesus' will.
You can meet them in school, or in lanes,
    or at sea,
in church, or in trains, or in shops, or at tea,
for the saints of God are folk just like me,
and I mean to be one too.[15]

You see, O Best Beloved, the God we believe in is the
God whose story we tell, in word and in action. The
truth is that sometimes I have done this well and sometimes I have not. But I try and I long to be a faithful fol-
lower of this God. I want to know the story of God,
and to tell it to others. I long to tell the story of the
saints and the sinners who have tried, failed, learned,
and tried again to follow God. And, in my daily life, I
hope to be just like the saints who have come before.

I have many years left in my ministry, but I can see a time years from now when someone will ask me, "Andy, what was it like when you first began?" I will tell them, "It was like a wilderness. People thought the church was dying, that the world was dying. People were hungry, and they were thirsty, and they needed a little hope, and they needed to believe in the future of the church and know that God had not abandoned them." And I will tell them, "But, people received the word of the Lord, and they picked up, and they went out into that wilderness, and they told that story. They told the one, true story. They told that sweet, sweet story. O Best Beloved, the Lord is good, and his mercy is everlasting. And it changed everything."

chapter four

The Gospel Fire

Celebrant	Do you believe in Jesus Christ, the Son of God?
Candidate	I believe in Jesus Christ, his only Son, our Lord. He was conceived by the power of the Holy Spirit and born of the Virgin Mary. He suffered under Pontius Pilate, was crucified, died, and was buried. He descended to the dead. On the third day he rose again. He ascended into heaven, and is seated at the right hand of the Father. He will come again to judge the living and the dead.[16]

I came to bring fire to the earth, and how I wish it were already kindled!

— LUKE 12:49

I love living in Texas. It is really hot, though. In recent years a number of droughts have increased the danger of fire, and large fires have devastated huge amounts of forest and fields.

A friend of mine gave me a book called *The Big Burn* by Stan Cohen and Donald Miller. It's about the great fire of 1910 that swept across Washington State, Idaho, and Montana. This fire scorched more than three million acres, and smoke could be seen in New York and in Colorado.[17]

The fire began within the first five years of the birth of the National Forestry Service. There were eighty-seven fatalities, twenty-five of whom were members of a team of servicemen who had been sent to stop the blaze from consuming a small town. This tragedy forever changed how we understand the management of national lands. The Forest Service began to focus its work on not only the prevention but also the management of forest fires.

Fire, we understand today, renews the forest. It builds diversity within the trees, recycles nutrients that lie barren on the forest floor and decreases diseases in plants. It destroys, creates, regenerates, recycles; and, in fact, some species depend on the fire to grow new seeds into trees. This is one of the many places where we see God's creative hand at work, and we still have much to learn from this process. What is there to learn? That we need not be wholly afraid of fire. That we must respect its power.

Man on Fire

Jesus understood fire. He was not afraid of fire. He regularly walked directly into it. He was a man on fire. That is why he announces in the Gospel of Luke:

> I came to bring fire to the earth, and how I wish it were already kindled! I have a baptism with which to be baptized, and what stress I am under until it is completed! Do you think that I have come to bring peace to the earth? No, I tell you, but rather division! From now on five in one household will be divided, three against two and two against three; they will be divided: father against son and son against father, mother against daughter and daughter against mother, mother-in-law against her daughter-in-law and daughter-in-law against mother-in-law. (Luke 12:49–53)

As Jesus is preaching and teaching, and the crowds continue to grow, he is offering a vision of the reign of God, a vision that breaks out of the captivity of temples, and breaks into the lives of people. I can imagine that some people are longing for the change he announces and others are threatened.

Imagine Jesus looking around, seeing families divided as some people choose to follow him and some do not. He knows that this will not necessarily be a peaceful journey, but he beckons us, nonetheless, to come with him into the fire—come with him to Jerusalem. Jesus never promises to his disciples or to any of those who seek to follow him that their journey

will be easy or that there will not be worldly conse-
quences for choosing to live in this new way. The fire
Jesus is speaking of is a refining fire that not only puri-
fies us, it changes us. The fire of Jesus burns in the
hearts of his disciples *and* changes their relationships
with the society around them. This fire Jesus hopes to
light in us is a baptismal fire.

John the Baptist tells us that while he baptizes with
water, another is coming to baptize with fire. The Baptismal Covenant is nothing short of a call to walk into
that fire. A friend once told me that it is easy to believe
in God, but once you begin to say you believe in Jesus,
you really begin to push the envelope. Making these
statements about faith does not mean that we have fig-
ured everything out. We do not reach stages of greater
or higher spiritual learning and thus become worthy of
God's grace. No, in our belief and in our disbelief, we
are part of the family of God. As the father of a dying
child once pleaded with Jesus, "I believe; help my un-
belief!" (Mark 9:24).

This leads to a question: "Are you ready?" Every
time we reaffirm our baptismal vows we are proclaiming, "I am ready to walk with God, and I am ready to
walk with Jesus." Every time a person is baptized in our
church or is confirmed, the whole community is reminded of its core faith. We are challenged by these
words, and we confirm the faith of the church and our
own faith every time. We say *yes* to Jesus, and we say
yes to walking with Jesus into the fire of transformation. Mind you, we have nothing to fear from this
gospel fire. Like Shadrach, Meshach, and Abednego,
who walked into the fire full of faith that God would
protect them (Daniel 1–3), I put my faith in God, too.

Walking into the Fire

As human beings, our natural response to fire is to stand back. From time to time curiosity might draw us closer. However, as soon as the heat begins to burn our faces, we move away.

Life is full of fires. Think about your relationships with family and friends, your tasks at work, school, or church. Think of the stress and problems to be solved. How do we describe addressing this mountain of responsibility? "Oh, I'm just putting out fires left and right." We, on our own, will handle the problem, douse the fires.

What about when the fires blaze too hot, when the smoke is so dense we cannot see clearly, when the problem is too big, the pain too sharp, the destruction too widespread? What do we do then? We're tempted to stand back, to turn and run.

Following Jesus into the fire is different. We are invited to trust that Jesus has already gone into the fires that burn before us and he is waiting for us there. We as followers of Jesus must trust that this man on fire is calling us to join him and that he will lead us through them. It is as if Jesus is saying, "Are you ready to be baptized as I am baptized? Are you ready to follow me into the fire?" (Mark 10:39).

When we choose Jesus, when we choose to follow this man, we make a clear and courageous choice. We choose to follow Jesus and to let the fires burn around us. We choose to be different, as he was different. Believing that Jesus was given life and ministry through

God's Spirit and that he suffered and died and was buried as part of a willingness to walk into the fires of death—this is not only courageous but it speaks to a radical turn in our lives, too. Claiming his story as our own, we come to understand that the fires of this world, not unlike the powers of this world, are of no consequence when measured against eternal life lived in Jesus Christ.

Our gaze is not merely on eternity, though. We can walk into the fire with Jesus today and live new lives *now.* We can live empowered by the same indwelling Spirit that Jesus possessed. This is in part due to our baptism and our daily prayer, both of which help to guide our living. We can choose to be servants of all and to share the good news of Jesus with those around us. We can choose to build homes for the homeless, to cook food for the hungry, to dismantle evil systems, to give from the bounty God has provided us. Sometimes the fire of these choices and the burning heat of this living will get too hot. But we know and understand as Episcopalians that, as we live out a transformed life, we are mirroring the life of Jesus. When we do this as individuals, we not only mirror the God we believe in, but we actually come closer into his presence.

Are we ready? The fire is burning all around us. The world itself is on fire. It is on fire with political unrest, economic inequality, and individual calamity. In many ways people all over the world are waiting to see who will come into the fire and walk with them. The world is burning and some may wonder: "Do these Christians, these Episcopalians, act out what they believe in, or is it simply more inflamed rhetoric? Do they believe in Jesus?" Jesus walked into the flames to heal the blind man. He walked into the flames to save the adulterous woman. He walked into the flames to feed a crowd of people who were hungry and thirsty, to still the stormy waters, to face down death on Good Friday. Can we follow him?

There is a poem called "A Man on Fire," written by Peter Ponzio as a reflection on a famous portrait of artist Vincent van Gogh. It reminds me of the opportunity, in this moment, to actually follow Jesus.

Red flames descend from the sky,
Burning into the depths of his eyes,
And crackle as they engulf his hair,
In tongues of fire.

The eyes, the eyes, stare out in
Placid indifference, while all around
Tongues of flame lick the air
Combusting in the night.

No stars here; no limned moon;
No serene reflections on the fiery
Pools below; only fire and burning,
And passion sleeping in those lidded eyes.

Saint or madman? Artist or lunatic?
Does it matter to a man on fire?
Can mere words express the desire
That fanned the flames into a conflagration,

And set the canvas alight? Oh, I long
For a flame to consume my desire,
To quench the thirst of my longing,
To plunge headfirst into the flames

That destroy all conscious thought,
All empty lies, all words written on
Cracked parchment. I long for the
Purity of fire, the peace of flames.[18]

Soaked in the waters of baptism, we become impervious to the fire. That's why baptism is so serious. We know that every child of God will encounter the fires of life: disappointment, heartache, injustice, sickness. But we also know Jesus Christ has promised to be with them, always. When a priest sprinkles water on that child or immerses that adult, when the priest hands over a taper lit from the Paschal candle, when we pray for those to be baptized, we are together proclaiming, "No harm will come to you. The fire of Christ will not burn you but will burn within you." Jesus and his church are gathered around us to hold our hands, as we stand together in this all-consuming fire of Christ.

chapter five

Steps Up the Mountain Path

Celebrant	Do you believe in God the Holy Spirit?
Candidate	I believe in the Holy Spirit, the holy catholic Church, the communion of saints, the forgiveness of sins, the resurrection of the body, and the life everlasting.[19]

And Jesus said to them, "Follow me, and I will make you fish for people." Immediately they left their nets and followed him.

— MATTHEW 4:19–20

In 1920, the thirteenth Dalai Lama gave special permission to the Mount Everest Committee of the Alpine Club at the Royal Geographical Society allowing access to climbers and surveyors, so that the surrounding region of Nepal could be mapped and climbed. Throughout the late 1920s and 1930s, the Society sent imperial-sized legions of British climbers, sherpas, and a city of support personnel to assault the great mountain, Sagarmatha, Goddess of the Sky, Everest.

In 1928, Hugh Rutledge was chosen to head that year's expedition, and he took with him a twenty-one-year-old woman, Christine Bond. She served as a nurse and traveled with his team through the Himalayan Mountains in Nepal. She was one of the first women mountaineers to navigate the Himalayas. She explored the previously unmapped upper reaches of Nepal, and Rutledge's team climbed to villages where they had never seen a white woman before. She wrote, "When I arrived, I didn't even have the right clothes at all. It was the beginning of climbing. We had to be given goggles and fitted with trousers made of some kind of tough material so they would last, and it took quite a long time to acclimatize and get used to the mountain region."[20]

The cold was not the only danger facing Himalayan explorers in the 1920s. When I first heard about Christine Bond, she was ninety-six years old and living in Hastings, England. She told the story of how one night when she was sleeping in her tent, a snow leopard prowled nearby. After the sherpas killed it with sticks, they gave the carcass to her because they thought she was such a brave English woman to have come all that way.

Of course, it would not be until 1953 that Sir Edmund Hillary ascended the top of Mount Everest and until 1975 that the first woman, Junko Tabei, reached the top. Nevertheless, Christine Bond was changed and formed by those years spent in Nepal, walking step by step up a treacherous road. That journey inspired the way she lived, and she would tell stories of snow leopards and faraway villages to her daughter and then to her granddaughter.

In 2004, seventy-five years and two generations later, Annabelle Bond, Christine's granddaughter, followed in her grandmother's footsteps and beyond. At thirty-four, Annabelle took on the toughest and most dangerous challenge in mountaineering. Inspired by her grandmother's stories, she attempted the seven summits. That feat, conquering the highest peak on each of the seven continents, has been accomplished by only 115 explorers in history. She completed the Seven Summits Challenge in 360 days, reaching the summit of Denali in Alaska on the 10th of May in 2005, making her the fastest woman climber in the world.[21]

Annabelle still climbs today. After climbing the seven summits, she continued to climb to raise money for the Eve Appeal, which specializes in the prevention of ovarian cancer. She has raised more than $1.6 million, and those dollars have saved the lives of many women. Annabelle was inspired to follow the footsteps of her grandmother, Christine.

When you take the first steps it is difficult to envision the culmination of your journey, or the impact those steps and the accompanying stories will have on those around you. It was probably tough for Christine to imagine, when she took those first steps all those years ago, that her stories and experiences would shape one of the finest mountaineering women in our history—her granddaughter.

An Unbroken Chain

Not unlike Annabelle and her grandmother, you and I walk in the footsteps of the Christian men and women who have gone before us as faithful followers of Jesus. Our spiritual parents and grandparents, the saints of God, passed to us what they received. Through the power of the Holy Spirit they shared in loving ways what they had been given, offering us the opportunity to follow in their footsteps. They did this in intentional ways to be sure, like when my grandmother taught me how to pray before I went to church. But they did it in unintentional ways, too, as when my grandfather took time in the evenings to sit and tell me stories. It is hard to recall all the people who have shaped my spiritual life, there are so many.

I have a great picture of my dad and his confirmation class, and in the foreground is a woman I only know as Deaconess Crow. Unknown to me, she must have shaped my father's spiritual life, which in turn shaped my life. I am sure that when my father, who was an Episcopal priest, sat down at our dining room table and prepared me to be confirmed, I was getting some of that deaconess' thoughts (though I assuredly did not know it at the time).

In our Episcopal Church we value these relationships. Within these connections there are bonds of affection that manifest God's love, and teachings that capture the meaning of our life with God. If we could picture them all, we would find they formed a link all the way back to the first followers of Jesus, who began their journey by entering into relationship with Jesus.

The Gospel of Matthew lays the story out for us. We encounter Jesus at a very important time in his ministry. He has just emerged from forty days in the desert, a private time of temptation and formation, and now he is setting out on his public ministry. He reaches the Sea of Galilee, and he sees two fishermen, two brothers casting their nets, and he says to them, "Follow me, and I will make you fish for people" (Matthew 4:18–20).

"Follow me" and "fish for people." Those words resound as the call to Christian discipleship. The interesting thing is that the word used here for "follow" is more accurately rendered "Come with me now. Don't delay." In other words, "The kingdom of God is at hand. Don't just follow me, but come with me. Walk in my footsteps right now." The immediacy of the call is clear, and they do just what he says, dropping their nets and following him. That is the power of Jesus' presence and of the Holy Spirit.

Then, Jesus puts flesh on the bones of his invitation: "Come and be fishers of men—be fishers of people." As Christians, we often understand these words in the sense of evangelism. We are to spread the gospel, to reach out. As the brothers dropped one net, they picked up another, in order to go fish for people. However, there is more to Jesus' choice of words than simply helping people find God. If you hunt for other uses of the term "to fish for people," they are rare and almost always associated with "call" stories—stories of vocation.

Having been schooled in the local synagogue, Jesus surely chose these words intentionally. In particular, I imagine he had an eye on the book of Jeremiah. The prophet proclaims his vision of a new kingdom where God will gather in all of Israel and says, "I am now sending for many fishermen, says the LORD, and they shall catch them; and afterward I will send for many hunters, and they shall hunt them from every mountain and every hill, and out of the clefts of the rocks" (Jeremiah 16:16). God is calling for fishermen and hunters to go find the scattered people, to pull them out of the caves and bring them home to the kingdom.

Nearly all the prophets—Amos, Habakkuk, Isaiah, Daniel, Elijah, Jonah, and more—tell us the kingdom of God is at hand and that there will be grace and plentitude there for everyone. Indeed, it must have been incredible for these Jewish men to stand at the Sea of Galilee, to hear Jesus' call to them, to recognize it as a prophet's call, to know that the Word was there on his lips and in their hearts. How powerful, to know that their work was not just to go get people. They were being offered an opportunity to be partners with God, to find those who had no home, those who felt lost, those who did not have anything, and to restore them all to God's family. They had only heard the stories, but now they heard the call to join God and bind up the brokenhearted and help the mournful to sing a new song and find the lost sheep of Israel.

It is the same for us. Jesus is here, offering the same invitation to drop everything and change the world. Go out and find the people. Be true fishers of souls who feel lost and left out.

People of the Spirit

Now, if we keep turning the pages of Matthew's gospel, we follow Jesus up to the mountaintop where he offers the Sermon on the Mount. He has moved from preparation in the desert, to calling the faithful few to join him on the prophet's errand. Then he begins his work, teaching the people of God our life's purpose, reminding humanity that we are created to glorify God and to pursue God's dream of reconciliation and restoration.

From the mount he challenges those with ears to truly listen. I hear him saying: "Blessed are the poor in spirit. These are the ones desperately yearning to hear the comfortable words from your lips. Blessed are those who hunger. These are your people. Blessed are those who thirst for righteousness. These are the ones I want you to seek and bring home." What are we to do? Love people. Offer them a vision of our journey walked with Christ. Tell them of our footsteps, the road we walk to heaven.

Think of those who have shared the vision of their work and, in turn, had an impact on your pilgrim journey. Who had the Word on their lips and in their hearts? Who offered you a bit of mercy and changed your life? In those moments when we were not sure about the future, they scooped us up in their nets, shared their life's work in Christ, and set us back on solid ground.

I know my life is different because of the people who chose, in a flash moment when I most needed them, to drop everything and be there for me. Late night conversations perched up on a dam with high school friends, solid figures who put their arms around me when my best friend died, generous ones who literally took me in and gave me shelter when I had no home—each of those good people said *yes,* and their yes to God in their ordinary lives shaped me and allowed me to take another step on the path.

Most of us will never travel to Nepal and conquer Mount Everest. We, like the fishermen, live ordinary lives, but we are given the opportunity to live those normal lives in an extraordinary manner. God invites us to come with him today, to follow in his footsteps, to be people of mercy and to be peacemakers along the road, and to fish and catch people. That is the work of the church, this communion of saints, this body knit together and filled with the Holy Spirit, walking up the path together to heaven.

We may not climb mountains, you and I, but if we have a little faith and the Word near us, on our lips and in our hearts, "as small as a mustard seed," we can move mountains. So keep the Word close. Walk in Jesus' footsteps. Let the Holy Spirit work in you. This is the church in the world today.

chapter six

Beginning and Continuing

Celebrant   Will you continue in the apostles'
teaching and fellowship, in the
breaking of bread, and in the prayers?

Candidate   I will, with God's help.[22]

For I am convinced that neither death, nor life, nor
angels, nor rulers, nor things present, nor things to
come, nor powers, nor height, nor depth, nor
anything else in all creation, will be able to
separate us from the love of God in Christ Jesus
our Lord.

— ROMANS 8:38–39

ife was not going well. It was the fall of 1999. I was serving as a mission priest in a parish deeply connected to Texas A&M University in College Station, and I felt trapped under the weight of my own ministry. I was young and eager and took on too much myself, refusing to share the load with the members. My relationship with my family was strained. I did not have a clergy group or group of confidants. My prayer life was in the dump.

And then came tragedy.

It was early morning, and I was driving to Austin from College Station. I received a phone call from a parishioner, informing me that the annual bonfire—a flaming wooden structure that towered some fifty feet in the air—had fallen, crushing and killing a number of students. I immediately turned my car around and found myself on site, ministering to traumatized young people and to police officers, firemen, and others engaged in the desperate rescue effort. It took all I had ... and more.

Thrust against the wall, sapped of my own power, I knew I couldn't go on as I had. Something had to change. Finding a counselor helped, and so did linking with a clergy group and a monastic community. I also entered Al-Anon, a group for family members of alcoholics, and began working the Twelve-Step Program.

Accompanied by a great sponsor, I was soon reading my copy of *One Day at a Time* and attending Al-Anon meetings regularly. I cruised through Step One: "We admitted we were powerless over alcohol—that our lives had become unmanageable." Step Two was a little harder: "We came to believe that a Power greater than ourselves could restore us to sanity." I could get that God was greater than I am, but depending on God to restore me? I struggled and held back, but eventually I realized I could trust God's power.

Then came Step Three: "We made a decision to turn our will and our lives over to the care of God as we understood Him." In this step I ran into a major stumbling block. I could do theology, preach, lead the Eucharist, and do all manner of priestly things, but could I turn my will and my life over to the care of God? Not the God I understood at the time.

I entered what some might call the dark night of the soul, that moment when a person discovers what he believes. And I wasn't ready. But one night, after a particularly difficult Al-Anon meeting, I went to the church and fell to my knees in prayer. I cried. I yelled at God. Finally, like one of our Texas thunderstorms, it passed over and I was quiet. In the stillness there came clarity. Beauty. Love like I had never known or experienced. Out of this pouring out and pouring in of the Holy Spirit I understood that when I gave up and rested in God, I received the gracious gift of sanity and clarity of vision.

I understood for the first time in my life God's love for me through Jesus Christ, and that there was nothing in heaven or under heaven, no power or authority that would or could separate me from God's love. There was no challenge too great that could not be seen through to its end because of God's love. There was no pain so deep that God's grace could not heal it. There was nothing that could prevent God's power from raising me up and giving me eyes to see the path of Jesus before me. I had preached it for years but only then, in the quiet of a little church in Texas, did I finally get it.

What I got was this: I had been pushing and striving and putting my work first, as if my efforts alone would save everyone, including myself. But prayer—the practice of turning our lives over to God's grace—*is* work, and work originates from prayer. Jesus taught it to his disciples, and those earliest followers shaped their communities around it: prayer and common meals first, then action. Prayer shapes our believing, as breaking bread with all kinds of people shapes our living.

God intends for us, through the Holy Spirit, to pray throughout our life and for our action to rise from our prayer and relationship with God.

The Discipline of Prayer

It's one thing to find a place for prayer, even a type of prayer. Doing it daily, not unlike exercise, is the difficult part. To maintain a life of prayer akin to breathing is every disciple's goal, yet it remains out of reach for most of us. In part, maintaining a healthy prayer life is difficult because we fall away so quickly. It is easy to let the day's interruptions take charge, and so we drift little by little away from a sustainable and sustaining routine. I encourage you to do this work. Identify a place, carve out a time, and commit. If you have tried it before, return to it yet again. Living in the fellowship of the saints is predominately a work of prayer. You will find it so much more difficult to engage in kingdom-building if you are not building on a strong foundation of prayer.

Being mindful and prayerful is not just something you do while locked away in secret. Prayer is for all of life, so have courage and bring prayer into yours. Feel free to pray in the car, in your office, at your dinner table, with your children, with friends, before a meeting, after a meeting. The Holy Spirit, which seeks to unite us with God, also opens our hearts and eyes to discover God in our world. Prayer tunes you to see and be aligned with the Spirit.

The Rule of the Society of Saint John the Evangelist (SSJE), an Episcopal monastic community of which I am a fellowship member, states that by praying throughout our life we see how we can "be available to God in the present moment." Over time, we see that "prayer comes to permeate our life and transfigure our mundane routines."[23] We are in some very real way, when we choose to follow Jesus, choosing not simply to learn to pray, but to pray as we live.

Karl Rahner, a major twentieth-century Roman Catholic theologian and one of the architects of the Second Vatican Council, prayed:

> I now see clearly that, if there is any path at all on which I can approach You, it must lead through the very middle of my ordinary daily life. If I should try to flee to You by any other way, I'd actually be leaving myself behind, and that, aside from being quite impossible, would accomplish nothing at all.[24]

Jesus' Prayer

In the Episcopal Church, the Lord's Prayer—the prayer Jesus taught his disciples—is central to our common life of prayer. It is present in all of our private and corporate services of worship, and is often the first prayer children learn. With the simplest of words, Jesus teaches those who follow him all they need to know about prayer.

Our Father

Our Father, because we are to seek as intimate a relationship with God as Jesus did. We can develop this intimate love with God, recognizing we are children of God and members of the family of God.

Who art in heaven

We are reminded of our created nature as a gift from heaven. Life is given to us from God, who is quite beyond us. We recognize in this short phrase that we are not God. Rather, the God we proclaim is a God who makes all things and breathes life into all things.

Hallowed be thy name

In response to the grace of being welcomed into God's community, bowing humbly and acknowledging our created nature, we recognize the holiness of God. We proclaim that God's name is hallowed.

Thy kingdom come

We ask and seek God's kingdom. The words of Jesus remind us that, like the disciples' own desires to sit at the right and left hand of Jesus, this is not our kingdom. The reign of God is not what you and I have in mind. We beg, "God, by your power bring your kingdom into this world. Help us to beat our swords into plough-shares that we might feed the world. Give us strength to commit as your partners in the restoration of creation, not how we imagine it, but in the way you imagine it."

Thy will be done

We bend our wills to God's, following the living example of Jesus Christ. We ask for grace to constantly set aside our desires and take on the love of God's reign. We pray, "Let our hands and hearts build not powers and principalities but the rule of love and care for all sorts and conditions of humanity. Let us have a measure of wisdom to tear down our self-imposed walls and embrace one another, as the lion and the lamb lay down together in the kingdom of God."

On earth as it is in heaven

We ask God to give us eyes to see this kingdom vision, and then we ask for courage and power to make heaven a reality in this world. We pray to God, "Create in us a will to be helping hands and loving hearts for those who are weary and need to rest in you. May our homes, our churches, and our communities be a sanctuary for the hurting world to find shelter, to find some small experience of heaven."

Give us this day our daily bread

In prayer we come to understand that we are consumers. We need, desire, and just want many things. In Christ, we are reminded that all we need is our daily bread. So we pray, "O God, help us to be mindful that you provide for the lilies of the field and you provide for us. As we surrender our desires, help us to provide daily bread for those who have none today."

Forgive us our trespasses, as we forgive those who trespass against us

Sanity and restoration are possible only because God forgives us. Because of that sacrificial forgiveness—

made real in the life and death of Jesus—we can see and then share mercy and forgiveness. Then we can pray, "God, may I understand your call to me personally to offer sacrificial forgiveness to all those I feel have wronged me. I want to know and see my own fault in those broken relationships. May I be the sacrament of your grace and forgiveness to others."

Lead us not into temptation

As Adam and Eve ate from the tree of knowledge and replaced God with their own understanding of reality, we need help turning away from our own earthly and political desires and turning toward the wisdom of God in Christ Jesus. So we ask, "We are so tempted to go the easy way, to believe our desires are God's desires. We have the audacity to assume we can know God's mind. Show us your way and help us to trust it."

Deliver us from evil

Only God can deliver us from evil. There is darkness in the world around us. We know this darkness feeds on our deepest desire: to be God ourselves. That deceptive voice affirms everything we do and justifies our actions, even when they compromise other people's dignity. It whispers and tells us we possess God's truth and no one else does. We must pray, "God, deliver us from the evil that inhabits this world, the weakness of our hearts, and the darkness of our lives, that we might walk in the light of your Son."

For thine is the kingdom, and the power, and the glory, for ever and ever. Amen.

Without God, we are powerless. So we devote our lives to God, resting in the power of God's deliverance. We humbly ask, "Help us to see your glory and beauty in the world, this day and every day. Amen."

Using prayers like this one, Jesus modeled a life of prayer as work, and work as prayer. The apostles and all those who have since followed him have sought a life of prayer. They have engaged in prayer that discerns Jesus' teachings and then molded their lives into the shape of his life. We can take up the same vocation and become people whose lives are characterized by daily and fervent prayer. Indeed we reflect and acknowledge the centrality of prayer and work in our own commitment to God when we say, "I will, with God's help, continue in the apostles' teaching and fellowship, in the breaking of bread, and in the prayers."

Entering God's Community

God is united in an infinite exchange of love: Father, Son, and Holy Spirit. This is the very simplest way of understanding the divine union we call the Trinity. So prayer is not, in its very nature, simply a conversation with God. When we pray, we participate in the divine life of love, the divine community, the divine conversation. As God's creatures we become entangled in the embrace of God.

Through prayer we are lifted into the community of God. In this embrace, the idea of praying to or worshiping a foreign or "distant" God disappears. We are overcome by the grace of being invited into the divine union of God, and as a result our own adoration and thanks-giving well up and pour out.

Prayer is sacramental—a visible, physical sign filled with an invisible grace, a tangible link between us and Jesus. In it we discover again and again that we are members of God's body, tied to both the community of the Trinity, and to the community of the faithful. When we pray, God hears the voice of Jesus in our prayers and accepts them as his own.

Especially when we bring intercessions for others to this communal God, we discover a deep and abiding kinship. I pray for my family, my friends, my cowork-ers, my clergy and parishioners. People give me their names and their causes because they know I pray for them. I pray for them by name, and I imagine their faces. I believe God is at work in these prayers, and that my voice is part of Christ's voice raising each person to God, my Father, who is in heaven.

Our prayers for those among us who are poor, wid-owed, sick, homeless, lonely, or lost bridge the chasm between us all and send us out, empowered by the Holy Spirit, to work for healing and reconciliation, forgive-ness and restoration. Our prayer also leads us to help people discover their own vocations. We are guides along the way, listening with people and helping them to listen for God as they discern their own unique call-ings into ministry.

As the SSJE Rule reminds us, "In praying for others we learn really and truly to love them. As we approach God on their behalf we carry the thought of them into the very being of eternal love and as we go into the being of him who is eternal Love, so we learn to love whatever we take with us there."[25] If we are following Jesus, then prayer must be the origin of our work. This is the way we come to know our place within the community of God. This is the way God's community comes alive on earth.

chapter seven

Turn, Turn, Turn

Celebrant Will you persevere in resisting evil, and, whenever you fall into sin, repent and return to the Lord?

Candidate I will, with God's help.[26]

Repent therefore, and turn to God so that your sins may be wiped out.

— ACTS 3:19

One Sunday in Texas I was visiting a small town church outside Austin. I was standing in the parish hall after church partaking in the eighth sacrament (coffee and doughnuts) and wearing my uniform: blue blazer and khaki pants, boots, and a Stetson. A nice woman walked forward, looked me up and down and declared, "Well, you haven't changed much."

I said, "Oh?"—surprised this stranger could so quickly take my measure.

With a twinkle in her eye, she continued, "Every night when I came to your house to babysit you, you were always wearing boots, a diaper, two six-guns, and a hat. I'm glad you don't have the six-guns anymore." I laughed and embraced my favorite old babysitter.

What she didn't know was that it took me a long time to come around to this "old" uniform. In 1976, ten years after she had moved on, I was wearing bell-bottom jeans and a silk shirt with birds all over it and a collar that came out to my shoulders. My hair was long, and I listened to Donna Summer and The Village People.

A few years later, *The Official Preppy Handbook* came out, calling for a cranberry-colored sports coat, khaki pants, and an $8 haircut. You could just call me "Chip."

The end of the 1980s found me in art school, wearing blue jeans filled with holes and splotches of paint (because I was, in fact, an art student). Add cowboy boots, lots of bandanas, several T-shirts all at the same time, and an earring.

I cleaned up for my first job, and by my Virginia Theological Seminary years I was in blue sports coat, khaki pants, a bow tie...and that same $8 haircut.

In the late nineties, I took a post at a church in College Station, and once again donned the long hair and the Birkenstocks—this time with khaki pants and a short-sleeved collared shirt. And now I am back to my boots, my blue blazer, and my Stetson. So I have come full circle.

Why this fashion autobiography? As we look back over our lives, we can see mistakes we have made along the way, and we make course corrections. We are trying to find our true selves, who God has created us to be, what God has created us to do. Along the way, we sin. We repent, we turn toward God again. The cycle never ends. Wash, rinse, repeat.

Getting Ready to Meet My Lord

In the Old Testament, you can always spot the prophets. Elijah had just pronounced a harsh judgment on King Ahaziah, after the king consulted Baal-zebub, the false god of Ekron, instead of the God of Israel. When the king's messengers brought word of the Lord's warning—"You shall not leave the bed to which you have gone, but you shall surely die"—the king asked what kind of man could possibly bear such terrible news. And the messengers answered, "A hairy man, with a leather belt around his waist." Then the king realized that the man was Elijah the Tishbite, who was a prophet (2 Kings 1:1–8).

When we get to the New Testament, we meet another hairy man in a camel hair shirt and a belt: John the Baptist. He appears in the wilderness of Judea—a dangerous, life-or-death place—and proclaims, "Repent, for the kingdom of heaven has come near" (Matthew 3:1–4).

Repent! We Episcopalians know about repentance. We repent on Sunday morning right after the Prayers of the People and before the announcements. But each of us brings a unique view of what repentance means. If you were a Roman Catholic before, you might have memories of regular private confession to a priest filling your head. If you were from a more Protestant denomination, you might remember altar calls to cleanse the sinner's soul. We place lots of baggage and assumptions on this word, "repentance."

In Greek, the word John the Baptist uses, though, is actually *metanoia*. *Metanoia* means "change": literally, to turn 180 degrees in the opposite direction. John is saying, "Change, because we must prepare the way for the Lord." The purpose of John's message is this. Number 1: "I am here to prepare you to meet Jesus." And Number 2: "I want you to be able to recognize him when he comes, and in order to do that, you have to change."

Just as the prophet Elijah spoke the truth to the king of Israel and called him to repentance, the prophet John speaks the truth, calling people to repent and prepare their hearts to receive living water. Just as King Ahaziah needlessly sought Baal-zebub, John told people they did not need the gods of the world around them; the gods of power and wealth, the gods of self-serving behaviors, and the gods of consumption were not going to save them. In response to John's message the people of Israel flocked to the Jordan River to find this new Elijah, and he met them out there, baptizing them and preparing them to meet their Lord.

A Life of Turning

The only way we can grow nearer to God is to continually and honestly face our sins and repent and return to the Lord. Think of the urgency of John's and Elijah's messages. Our life depends upon this change.

As I look back over my spiritual journey, I can see the sinful behaviors I have tried on and worn throughout my life. Over time I have learned that healing and redemption can only happen when I am attentive to my own weakness and disorder. Then the real opportunity for *metanoia* emerges. That's why, at the beginning of each day, I open the Prayer Book, do the Daily Office, and ask God to help me be changed. I have a long list of behaviors that need to change; I offer that list to God.

For instance, I ask the Lord to change my sarcastic attitude toward my life and relationships into a joyful one. I ask God to change my cynicism about the world into hope. I ask God to take my self-interest and change that into thoughtfulness, mindfulness, and compassion for others. I ask God to take my consumer nature and change it into a giving nature. I ask that my own sense of self-preservation would be changed by God's grace to complete dependence on him. That's just the short list of my sins, the ones most present to me. That is what I pray for.

As a church we pray for the grace to turn to new ways, as well:

Gracious Father, we pray for thy holy Catholic Church. Fill it with all truth, in all truth with all peace. Where it is corrupt, purify it; where it is in error, direct it; where in any thing it is amiss, reform it. Where it is right, strengthen it; where it is in want, provide for it; where it is divided, reunite it; for the sake of Jesus Christ thy Son our Savior. Amen.[27]

The Episcopal Church is a reformed church and that means that we understand that we are not perfect. Our Anglican tradition was born out of the suffering, persecution, and martyrdom of Roman Catholics and Protestants, and we do not hide from that fact. We remember that the wealth of many in these United States (including a disproportionate number of Episcopalians) was built and borne on the backs of slaves. We remember that much of our wealth was built on the backs of children, men, and women who worked in deplorable conditions in factories owned and operated by some Episcopalians during the Industrial Revolution. We cannot ignore sex scandals and abuse by clergy. We have to recall how we as a church have mistreated and continue to mistreat whole groups because of their ethnicity or gender.

I say all of this because one of the beautiful things about the Episcopal Church is our willingness to constantly try, by God's grace, to be better. We recognize we can be at war with ourselves, treat each other poorly, that we can be corrupt, we can be in error, and we can be faithless as a community. Every community has these traits; I am happy to be in a church that wrestles with its own sin and tries to live anew.

The Grace to Change

Christianity in the Episcopal tradition is a life practiced. Baptism is not a single stop at the River Jordan to put on our protective garments of baptism, after which we're covered. Neither will the church be perfected in our lifetime. Just as I harm others, so does the institution. Past and present, we have no doubt harmed others and sinned against God as we have made our all-too-human pilgrimage toward God's kingdom.

But we are on a journey. As individuals and as a corporeal institution we are seeking to love and follow Jesus. What I find in my journey is that, as I ask for grace to change, the Lord comes to me in people, in things I read, in the landscape around me. While I cannot go to the River Jordan, I can go to Eucharist every Sunday, and the sacrament of Christ's body and blood helps me to change.

The baptismal question is not, "*If* you sin, will you repent?" The question is, "*When* you sin, will you repent and return to the Lord?" The fact that you, that I, that everyone sins, is a given. It is our nature. The question is, will you turn? Will you change? Will you prepare in your heart the way of the Lord?

chapter eight

Don't Hold Back

Celebrant   Will you proclaim by word and
example the Good News of God in
Christ?

Candidate   I will, with God's help.[28]

Then Jesus came from Galilee to John at the
Jordan, to be baptized by him. John would have
prevented him, saying, "I need to be baptized by
you, and do you come to me?" But Jesus answered
him, "Let it be so now; for it is proper for us in this
way to fulfill all righteousness." Then he
consented. And when Jesus had been baptized,
just as he came up from the water, suddenly the
heavens were opened to him and he saw the Spirit
of God descending like a dove and alighting on
him. And a voice from heaven said, "This is my
Son, the Beloved, with whom I am well pleased."

— MATTHEW 3:13–17

In 1999, I trained to run the Austin Marathon, which I am proud to say I completed. One day I was out by myself for a long run. It was early and the streets were deserted. On this particularly windy day, I was struggling to pound out the miles.

I came up a long, straight stretch of road, and as I did so I noticed a man walking in the distance, coming toward me. He was wearing a dirty, torn up jacket, a woolen cap, and some old leather gloves. He was pulling what appeared to be an airport carry-on suitcase, and it looked like he might be carrying everything he owned.

While I was still some distance away, the man stopped and began to unload his gear. He sat most of it in a neat pile and then bent over and fiddled with it for a while. Just as I came even with him and began to pass, I realized he was pulling a speaker on wheels. What had he pulled out? A microphone. As I passed him he shouted through the amplifier: "Go! Go! Go!!" I waved and passed him with a huge smile on my face and a quickened pace that carried me the many miles ahead.

What I want to do is encourage you, to say to you: "Go! Go! Go!!" I want to ask you to keep running and, when the time comes, to pass good news along to others.

Moving God's Plan Forward

This chapter began with the story of Jesus' baptism. He came from Galilee to the Jordan to be baptized by his cousin John, but John tries to stop Jesus. He essentially bows to Jesus and says, "I'm not worthy. You should be the one baptizing me." John is apparently struck with this sense of urgency combined with an even bigger sense of inadequacy. That's why he says, in effect, "Stop!"

To be precise, in Greek the word John uses is more like he intends not just to "stop" Jesus but "to hold him back." Jesus won't be stopped. Even as John hesitates, Jesus insists: "You are worthy. I need you to do this so we can all move forward." Sure enough, after Jesus has been baptized the heavens open up, the Spirit descends like a dove, and a voice declares, "This is my Son, the Beloved, with whom I am well pleased" (Matthew 3:17).

What is Jesus trying to move forward? Nothing short of God's plan for the reconciliation of heaven and earth.

In the Genesis creation account, there is the realm where God lives, then there are the "firmaments," the water-like masses that God held back in order to create the earth. In our baptismal story Jesus rises out of the waters of the Jordan, and the heavens—the firmaments—are opened. But instead of marking separation, this time the heavens open up and all is connected. Instead of a creation story that establishes divisions all the way up to the abode of God, this is like a re-creation moment when things once divided can now merge into one.

Through Jesus Christ, the heavens are opened to us. Jesus breaks through every division and unites us with God. God does a new thing in us. We are a new creation. "If anyone is in Christ, there is a new creation: everything old has passed away; see, everything has become new!" (2 Corinthians 5:17). Matthew returns to this image again when Jesus dies and the temple curtain, which had separated worshippers from God here on earth, was torn in two (Matthew 27:50–51).

The mission of Jesus was to re-create the world by encouraging us to join him in the proclamation of the Good News of salvation and reconciliation with God. He came to remake the world, using the hands and voices of a united human community. We are co-creators in the work of mission and proclamation. He has called us and says, "Go! Go! Go!!"

Remade for Mission

You and I are re-created as we come to know Jesus. That re-creation is made real in the baptismal waters through which we make our journey. But for what purpose? Not unlike the work of Jesus, you and I have been brought into the family of God for the purpose of encouraging others, to help others along their journey, to make their steps a little lighter and their pace a little quicker, so that all may run the race closer to the kingdom of God.

As Christians, and specifically as Episcopalians, we have chosen to follow Jesus Christ. We say, "I am intentionally, week after week, day after day, going to try to place myself in relationship with Jesus so that my life and my story may be re-created." We strive to embody that re-creation throughout our lives. We are baptized and marked as Christ's own forever, and we are sent into the world to connect the realms of God—to re-create and make all things new. Church is one community where we connect with this story. We hear the Word opened up and participate in Eucharist. In these and so many other ways, we are fed and re-created.

Often times the Christian community is so focused on the individual in the baptism rite, we do not say much about our calling into kingdom work, the ministry of reconciliation and re-creation. Yet, Episcopalians live in particular mission contexts where we are responsible, with Jesus, for making the world over again in the shape of the reign of God.

If we look at the end of the Gospel of Matthew, Jesus calls his followers to go and make disciples of all nations, baptizing them in the name of Father, Son, and Holy Spirit, and teaching them his commandments (Matthew 28:19–20). On the one hand, we are to be re-created in community and worship; we are also called into the world, like Elijah, John, and the other prophets, to baptize, make disciples, teach commandments, mold and form servants and lovers of God. That is our work.

In our beloved Episcopal Church, more often than not, we step back from this extraordinary calling. We demur and say, "Oh no. Surely that's Jesus' work, not ours. Who are we to mold, to re-create, to partner in kingdom work?" Just like John, we want to hold back and not claim our ministry. We say, "We are not like those other churches. We do not ask total strangers if they have accepted Jesus Christ as their personal Lord and Savior. We are Episcopalians. Those whom God wants to be Episcopalians will find and join us."

Don't misunderstand me. That kind of thinking is the flip side of a real gift we Episcopalians possess: true humility about our relationship with God. We are a very prayer-oriented people, and on balance we are uncomfortable taking on the work of proclamation. Who are we to assume we could form another person's relation-

ship with God? Only God can do that, so let's leave it
between the person and God. While this impulse is sin-
cere and in some ways true, it may become an excuse
for not engaging in proclamation. We, like many Episcopalians before us, must remember it is "both/and"—
both personal prayer *and* public proclamation and
mission.

We proclaim the gospel by word, which is the sharing of the story of Jesus' life, crucifixion, death, resurrection, and ascension. We also proclaim the gospel in
our deeds. It is not enough to give people the living
word and the sacramental bread of life; we as Episcopalians believe real bread matters, too. To do one without the other is to deny our calling. One-time Bishop of
Texas and Presiding Bishop John Hines said it so well:

> Authentic evangelism is no specialized, separable or
> periodic activity of the called people of God. Rather
> is it a pervasive dimension of the total nature and
> activity of the church. Everything that the church is
> and does is of evangelizing significance. Where it is
> faithful it mirrors the one we call Lord and God.
> Evangelism only exists where there is social concern.
> Its only justification and reason for being lies in that
> decisive calculation: "For God so loved the
> world...." It resonates passionately to the late Dag
> Hammarskjöld's accurate observation, "The road to
> holiness passes directly through the world of ac-
> tion."

Expressed another way, there is no first moment of
love of God that is later followed by a love of one's
neighbor. As the Gospel is announced and received,
there is thy neighbor. If we persist in describing the
comfortable blessings that follow upon accepting

Jesus Christ as Lord, without both describing and demonstrating the demands that Christian discipleship mandates, we deceive the hearer and betray the Gospel.[29]

The Episcopal leaders who shaped our church and our nation did so because they had been formed in a church that was demanding and mission-oriented, a church that understood its work as shaping the culture in which it was embedded. In Matthew's gospel it is clear that the new church's mission was to welcome people into Christian community and help them re-shape their lives and the life of the world around them. The same words he spoke at the close of Matthew's gospel, Jesus speaks to us now: "If you are going to follow me, this is the way it is supposed to be. You go out. You baptize. You make disciples. You do the teaching. You create the body of Christ. You make the whole world new. Join me. Let's go!"

It's Time to Go

As you encounter people in your life at school or at work, at the grocery store or on an airplane, wherever it is, you might wonder, "Is this an opportunity to reach out, to begin that process of relationship-building that may lead to baptism? Might this person have a misunderstanding of what it means to be a Christian? Or might they not know who Jesus is at all?" You are being given countless opportunities to welcome people to find their way to the River Jordan, to the waters of baptism.

When you do, you are welcoming them to be re-created and to take on life and ministry as baptized Christians.

Don't hold back as John did. Share your faith journey and listen to the faith journey of others, and help them to discover re-created life in Christ. Proclaim by word and example the transformative news of Jesus, and take your part with him in changing the world.

There are people in your life today who are making their way towards you. They can see you from a distance. They are perhaps weary. Some may be far away from home. Others as they come closer are looking for help. Perhaps they have been running the race for a long time, clocked a lot of hours, and most of it alone. Maybe they are hoping for some encouragement, hope, and a reason to keep going. You and I as partners of Jesus can show up when their steps begin to flag. We can smile and say to them, "Don't stop now. Go! Go! Go!!"

chapter nine

The Table Is Now Made Ready

Celebrant	Will you seek and serve Christ in all persons, loving your neighbor as yourself?
Candidate	I will, with God's help.[30]

The kingdom of heaven may be compared to a king who gave a wedding banquet for his son. . . .

— MATTHEW 22

When my daughter Zoë was about six years old she was very excited about her upcoming birthday. She and I had this conversation:

Zoë: Well, Dad, you know—I really—you know—my bicycle is pretty small for me, and—you know—I am really good at it. I mean riding my bicycle. We have been practicing, a lot, haven't we, Dad?

Me: Yup, we sure have.

Zoë: (quiet for a moment) Um, when is my birthday?

Me: Well, it is in six weeks.

Zoë: Okay, well—Dad, you know—I am doing really well at school, and I was just wondering. . . . when is my birthday?

Me: It is in about a month and a half.

Zoë: Ohhh, okay, right, right.

(Pause)

Me: Zoë, your birthday is the day after my consecration to be a bishop.

Zoë: Ohhhh, okay, right.

So, we talk a little bit longer about school and other things. Then:

Zoë: Dad, you know—I want to just be—I'm hoping that we are going to have a little party for my birthday.

Me: Yes, we are having a party, and Nanny and Papa and Pops and Honey, and lots of your friends

and our friends, in fact everybody is coming, and it
will be a big party for you.

(Pause)

Zoë: And when is that, Dad?

Me: Zoë, it is in six weeks. It is November 23rd. It
is right before Thanksgiving and right after I am
made a bishop. Okay?

Zoë: Okay, Dad.

*(Silence from the back of the car except for the
sound of the wheels in her head turning.)*

Zoë: Yup. That bike sure is too small for me. Um,
Dad, when are you becoming a bishop?

The truth is everybody loves a good party. And when
it's a party for you, the anticipation is almost too much.
When will it be? Who gets to come? What will I get?
Like an innocent six-year-old, it's all about me.

The Wedding Banquet

Parties and grand occasions were not unfamiliar to the
author of the Gospel of Matthew, and as I reflect on our
particular ministry, I think of the wedding story Jesus
told to his disciples. Jesus unfolds the parable in this
way:

> The kingdom of heaven may be compared to a king
> who gave a wedding banquet for his son. He sent
> his slaves to call those who had been invited to the

wedding banquet, but they would not come. Again he sent other slaves, saying, "Tell those who have been invited: Look, I have prepared my dinner, my oxen and my fat calves have been slaughtered, and everything is ready; come to the wedding banquet." But they made light of it and went away....

Then he said to his slaves, "The wedding is ready, but those invited were not worthy. Go therefore into the main streets, and invite everyone you find to the wedding banquet." Those slaves went out into the streets and gathered all whom they found, both good and bad; so the wedding hall was filled with guests.

But when the king came in to see the guests, he noticed a man there who was not wearing a wedding robe, and he said to him, "Friend, how did you get in here without a wedding robe?" And he was speechless. Then the king said to the attendants, "Bind him hand and foot, and throw him into the outer darkness, where there will be weeping and gnashing of teeth." For many are called, but few are chosen. (Matthew 22:2–5, 8–14)

Many of Jesus' parables can make us anxious, and this is one of them. Like a six-year-old bursting with hope for a two-wheeler bike with a banana seat and streamers flowing from the handlebars, we want to know, "Am I getting in to Jesus' party? Am I even invited to the party?" And given the harsh turn the parable takes, we may also wonder, "If I go to the party, will I be welcomed? Does the kingdom include me?"

Tempting as this self-focus can be, it can become an obsession. Anglican theologian N. T. Wright helps to redirect our attention in his book *Surprised by Hope,* where he explains that the question, "Which human beings will God take to heaven?" isn't the right one to ask. Rather, we should wonder "how God is going to redeem and renew his creation through human beings."[31]

Look at this story closely. Jesus says, "The kingdom of heaven may be compared to a king who gave a wedding banquet for his son." The focus is on God and the banquet for God's son. The first readers of this gospel would have understood that this is Jesus' banquet.

The king sends his servants to call all those who had been invited, and not just that. The Greek word used here—*keklhmenous*—implies that these guests were invited and RSVP'd "Yes."[32] Now the king is sending his servants to let them know the banquet is ready, but they do not come.

Fourth-century bishop John Chrysostom has written about this same passage, and he believes this first group of servants is perhaps those early prophets—Isaiah, Amos, and many more—who also found that the guests to whom they called would not come.[33] But God remained faithful, sending servants out again and again: "Go out into the main streets. Do not stop with the ones who were invited—the ones who were chosen. Go out into the main streets and gather everybody. My people are hungry, and this huge banquet is for all of them."

Successive generations of servants obeyed; according to the parable, they "went out into the streets and gathered all whom they found, both good and bad." They did not stop to find out whether the good or the bad should be there. These servants, these vessels of grace sent out into the world to proclaim that the banquet feast was ready, understood that everybody was to receive what they offered. If you are invited and you send your RSVP, you better show up. But if you never received an official invitation, then God is sending friends to come and find you.

How often in our church communities do we extend that kind of invitation? More often, we wonder about the guests' past, their social class, their cultural background. We wonder, "Are they *our* people?" We live in a free country, and we have used that freedom to choose to be divided. Blue State versus Red State. Christian versus Muslim. Creationists versus Darwinists. Pro-life versus pro-choice. Gay versus straight. Poor versus rich. Those who think like us versus those who do not. This epidemic has infiltrated Christian communities, too. Some of us are invited and we stand against those who surely are not.

It's hard for us to accept the gift of the banquet and the breadth of God's invite list. But the servants were not stymied. They went out, and they brought in everyone. Everyone.

All that inclusivity seems to grind to a halt at the end of the parable, when we come to the most troubling section. The Lord singles out one man. "Friend, how did you get in here without a wedding robe?" Modern ears might interpret this as a criticism of his shoddy clothes. "Well, perhaps the man was too poor to wear the proper clothes. How can he be punished for that?"

Actually, the language of "wedding robe" had a very particular meaning for the early church; they would have known it was a reference to resurrection life. If the guest had no wedding robe, no resurrection garments, it meant he was not committed to the resurrection work of going out and gathering everyone. It is almost as if there is an exclamation point, in case we didn't get it the first time. You are not only invited to attend, but you must also be part of the community, prepared to literally usher in those who come after you.

When we read the parable, we naturally identify with the ones who have been judged: those who do not show up or the one without the right clothes. In reality, Jesus may be saying we are servants of the Most High God, who have been sent out again and again to find people, share the banquet with them and welcome them to share in resurrection life.

The Kingdom Is for All People

What the early Christians understood so clearly was this: the kingdom of God was a partnership between them and God. They knew their role was to go out, walk with people, and welcome them in. To seek and serve Christ in them. To treat them with the same compassion and forgiveness God had given them through Jesus Christ. To dismantle the walls of division and to know that those who were not previously part of their community were now their brothers and sisters in this emerging family of God.

You and I are the beneficiaries of that understanding. The church we receive today, the global church of which the Episcopal Church is a member, all came into being because faithful people answered a call. They went out, took the banquet to the streets and said, "The kingdom of God is now. Come and let us feast. Everyone put on your wedding garments, come and join us in inviting the whole of the world into the family of God."

That is our charge, as well. It's not about my bike, my party, my church, my liturgy. It's God's party, and we are God's partners in throwing it. The Episcopal Church has not always done well at sharing the good news, but over the years we have struggled to live as if our church—God's church—is for everyone. This zeal for mission and inclusion is our inheritance from the earliest followers of Jesus. That's why we can boldly proclaim in our Baptismal Covenant that we are to seek and serve Christ in all persons, loving our neighbor as ourselves.

We are invited to take up this work, knowing God has called us into partnership through baptism. God is beckoning us to go forth and meet the needs of our global neighborhood. Our business is restoring, with God and by the power of the Holy Spirit, a creation cloaked in corruption and chaos. This is the wedding garment we put on in our baptism. If we say *yes,* if we accept the banquet invitation, then discipleship follows.

The good news is that this *is* a partnership. We are not to save the world by ourselves. We are only to help God save the world. God equips us, every time we gather at the banquet table and receive the body and blood of Jesus Christ. Because of that meal we have the strength to go back into the streets, week after week, year after year, and proclaim the invitation. When people reject the invitation, we come back to be fed and strengthened and sent out once again. Episcopalians, like the servants in the parable, do not give up. We are a tenacious breed, and we seek to generously extend the invitation to participate in the kingdom of God.

Generous Inviting

My daughter Zoë had her party. She did get the bicycle. Everyone was there...including some unexpected guests. We all love a good party, a grand occasion, a wedding banquet. And perhaps the best news is that, for Episcopalians, we understand that the time is now. The banquet has begun. The kingdom of God is already in our midst. We are vessels of grace welcoming everyone to share at God's table, which is resplendent with all that we need to heal this ailing world. All we need to do now is go out into the streets and generously invite our neighbors to the feast.

When I was in parish ministry I loved the following invitation to communion, which I adapted from the Iona Community in Scotland. In my mind it captures the missionary spirit of the Episcopal Church:

> The table is now made ready.
> It is the table of fellowship with Jesus and all those
>   who love him.
> It is the table of fellowship with the poor and
>   hungry and those with whom Jesus identified.
> It is the table set in the midst of the world that
>   God loved and in which Christ was
>   made incarnate.
> So come to the table, come to the heavenly
>   banquet.
> Come, those of you who have much faith
>   and those of you who are seeking more.
> Come, those of you who have been to this feast

often and those who have not been
in a long time.
Come, those of you who have tried to follow Jesus
but believe you have failed.
Come, the wedding feast is now made ready.
It is the feast of Jesus and he invites us all to meet
him here.[34]

chapter ten

The Man at the Gate

Celebrant   Will you strive for justice and peace
among all people, and respect the
dignity of every human being?

Candidate   I will, with God's help.[35]

Peter said, "I have no silver or gold, but what I
have I give you; in the name of Jesus Christ of
Nazareth, stand up and walk."

— ACTS 3:6

al Raines is a political columnist and a fly fish-erman. Like a lot of people who learn how to fish, he had a father figure who showed him the way. For Hal, that man was Dick Blaylock. Dick took him to nearby streams, and after a while he noticed Hal was deeply frustrated because he wasn't catching any fish. Wasn't that the whole point? He had not yet learned the old adage that it isn't called "catching," it's called "fishing." Like most human beings, Hal liked being productive.

His teacher understood that instinct, so he gave him some glow bugs for easy short-term wins. Glow bugs are small, round, pill-like bugs, typically in a funny flu-orescent color, and you put a hook on the end and throw them in the water. Fish find them irresistible. Well, Hal caught tons and tons of fish. It was close to the miraculous haul of fish caught by the disciples and Jesus.

Feeling like the professional fisherman, he went off to Pennsylvania with his sons and said, "Guys, Uncle Dick taught me how to fish, and now let me show you." He and his sons caught mountains of fish with these glow bugs. He went back to Dick and said, "In Penn-sylvania we caught tons of fish." Dick asked how. "Glow bugs," Hal told him. Dick just replied, "Oh." Hal was flabbergasted. "What do you mean, 'Oh'?" Dick said, "Nothing really. It's just that those trout grow up in ponds, farm raised. They think glow bugs are the chow thrown out there at feeding time. You know, I just don't need to catch fish that bad anymore."

Hal didn't get it yet. "Well, why did you start me on glow bugs?" Dick said, "I thought you had to do it that way. You have to catch fish in order to learn how to fish."[36]

In that moment, I believe Hal realized that what matters is not how many you catch, but how you fish.

The same is true for us. Our actions really do speak louder than our words, our process more than our finish. When Jesus called the fishermen to follow him and fish for people, it mattered how they went about fulfilling their mission. The actions of the Christians and Episcopalians who claim to follow Jesus matter. At the end of every day in the kingdom of God, our baptismal actions speak louder than our baptismal promises.

It Matters How You Live

Jesus told this story to explain the importance of our actions:

> There was a rich man who was dressed in purple and fine linen and who feasted sumptuously every day. And at his gate lay a poor man named Lazarus, covered with sores, who longed to satisfy his hunger with what fell from the rich man's table; even the dogs would come and lick his sores.

> The poor man died and was carried away by the angels to be with Abraham. The rich man also died and was buried. In Hades, where he was being tormented, he looked up and saw Abraham far away with Lazarus by his side. He called out, "Father Abraham, have mercy on me, and send Lazarus to dip the tip of his finger in water and cool my tongue; for I am in agony in these flames." But Abraham said, "Child, remember that during your lifetime

you received your good things, and Lazarus in like manner evil things; but now he is comforted here, and you are in agony. Besides all this, between you and us a great chasm has been fixed, so that those who might want to pass from here to you cannot do so, and no one can cross from there to us."

He said, "Then, father, I beg you to send him to my father's house—for I have five brothers—that he may warn them, so that they will not also come into this place of torment." Abraham replied, "They have Moses and the prophets; they should listen to them." He said, "No, father Abraham; but if someone goes to them from the dead, they will repent." He said to him, "If they do not listen to Moses and the prophets, neither will they be convinced even if someone rises from the dead." (Luke 16:19–31)

There is a man at the gate and it matters how we treat him. It matters to the man, it matters to Jesus, and most of all it matters to God. It matters how the wealthy man treats Lazarus specifically and how the rich treat the poor generally. Day after day, as he passed through the gates, the rich man paid no attention to Lazarus. God, on the other hand, has a special concern for the man at the gate.

Jesus makes it clear that, if we love him, he expects us to care for those who have been abandoned, marginalized—for the sheep who have no shepherd. Remember the questions the resurrected Christ asked Simon Peter:

"Simon, son of John, do you love me more than these?"…Peter felt hurt because he said to him the third time, "Do you love me?" And he said to him,

"Lord, you know everything; you know that I love you." Jesus said to him, "Feed my sheep." (John 21:15, 17)

True, we are responsible for ourselves. But what the parable and the passage teach, which is radical, is that we are also responsible for the people in our lives and in the world around us. That is a hard message to hear. I am responsible for myself, and, to a lesser extent, I am responsible for my family. I have responsibilities at work; I can reach out and help people. But does God really expect me to be responsible for the man at the gate? Why? And how?

This work is more than just the rich tending the poor, though that is certainly part of it. Caring is often seen as something the "haves" do for the "have nots." But Jesus' challenge to us all is one that goes far beyond *noblesse oblige,* the condescending acts of the nobility on behalf of the poor. The radical message here is that we care for each other, I for you and you for me. This moves us beyond the notion of a Samaritan helping out a beaten and abandoned neighbor or a rich man helping out a poor man. On the contrary, Jesus' message is that we are now part of a radically reconfigured family wherein each one is a brother and sister for whom we are responsible.

Through the cross, Jesus has taken on responsibility for us, for the whole world. Now he needs us to do the same, to take up our cross and follow, and care for the world in which we live. That makes us responsible for our communities, our cities, our states, our nation, other nations, even our enemies. All the sheep are our responsibility.

Not just the ones who are like us.

Not just the ones who go to our church.

Not just the other Episcopalians.

Not just the Christians.

The hard lesson here, one we are all too eager as sinful broken human beings to ignore, is that it matters to God how we live and how we care for and stand with others. There is someone standing at the gate of our lives. And that person, that community, is waiting for us to stand with them as extensions of God's mercy, grace, and abundant love.

Luke is thoughtful enough to realize this message can sound harsh and demanding; thankfully, he also sends a message of hope. Luke believes that once you choose to follow Jesus, the power of the Holy Spirit sweeps in and incredible things are suddenly possible. You can take up your cross. You can tend and feed neighbors near and far. Luke knows we can reflect the goodness and grace of the God who made and redeemed us. Because of the Spirit's power pulsing at the heart of Christian community, we can take up our responsibility for one another, and share our lives for the glory of God.

Good and Dangerous News

In the Acts of Apostles, Luke provides yet another story of Christians who act out of deep care and solidarity with the suffering.

This time, the disciples Peter and John were on their way into the temple and saw a man at the gate. Every day his friends brought him to the gate of the temple, called the Beautiful Gate, hoping he would be cured, healed, or at least receive some measure of kindness.

The man at the gate reached out to Peter and John. Peter told him, "I have no gold or silver, but what I have I give you; in the name of Jesus Christ of Nazareth, stand up and walk." Then Peter takes his hand, raises him up, and sends him leaping and praising God on his way into the temple (Acts 3:1–8).

You and I offer a unique witness to God's plan for the salvation of the world through Jesus Christ. There is no theme, no hopeful message, no political agenda more transformative than the good news of salvation in Jesus Christ. We as Christians know a source of real healing for a hurting world; we have access to transformation for people in dire physical and spiritual need.

You and I are not in the business of persuading others of the truth of the gospel story through propositional argument. As Anglican theologian John Milbank claims, we are not about conversion through arguing about beliefs, which often becomes an act of violence against others.[37] We are rather about the work of "outnarrating" the world around us. By this, I simply mean there are rival narratives about what the world is, who God is, whether God is. We need to claim our unique proclamation of the greatest story there is to tell.

We as Christians can live out our faith so that others are attracted by the sublime beauty of God reflected in the church at work in the world. We, the church, are called to be what theologian Stanley Hauerwas calls a "community of character," embodying a "peaceable kingdom."[38] We are called to exhibit in our corporate life the radical alternative life of those who follow Christ. At baptism, we are marked with this sacred story on our foreheads, and thus marked as Christ's own forever. Hands are laid upon us by a bishop at confirmation and sometimes at reception into the Anglican Communion to empower us by the same Holy Spirit for a life of discovery, formation, and mission.

Like Peter and John, we have received the sacred story of transformation, of sin and redemption, death and resurrection, sickness and healing. Each one of the saints that has come before us has passed the narrative to us. Over the centuries the proclamation of this good news of salvation has out-narrated the secular world's story of hopelessness. Thousands of Christian saints, from Saint Peter Abelard with his poetry to Saint Francis with his actions, have proclaimed and given voice to the story, "that after his resurrection Jesus ascended into heaven and at the end of the age he will come in glory to judge the living and the dead and to finally and fully manifest the kingly rule of God over all of creation."[39]

As Episcopalians we go further, making a unique proclamation of the Christian faith. Several themes are at the heart of this uniquely Episcopal proclamation of the good news, and we share these convictions globally with other Anglicans. They are captured in the bedrock of our Baptismal Covenant. They guide our living of the gospel message:

1. Our Episcopal faith is supported by our continued reflection on Scripture, the apostles' teachings, communal prayer, and life lived in connection with the sacraments.

2. Mission is the work of God, who was sent into the world and sends us into the world. When we enact the gospel, we make Jesus Christ incarnate in the world. Mission and outreach are about Jesus: first, last, and always.

3. Mission and outreach are holistic. We seek to meet the needs of the whole person, spiritual and physical.

4. We proclaim in voice and in action the good news of the reign of God.

5. We teach, baptize, and nurture believers.

6. We respond to human need by serving others.

7. We transform unjust structures of society.

8. We seek sustainable and renewing initiatives that redeem not only humanity but the creation in which we live.

9. Our outreach and mission are always rooted in Scripture, tradition, and reason.

10. We make a greater witness to the world around us when we join hands with one another beyond differences of theology, ideology, and identity, in order to meet the human needs around us.

11. We are changed by serving and walking with others. We are incomplete without the poor, voiceless, and oppressed by our side.

12. We are saved and given power to serve and act only by God's grace.

This is the unique story of our faith. It is the rock upon which my life rests. It is the particular story which gives meaning to the chaos of a world ruled by powers and principalities. It is what we have been given by Jesus of Nazareth and what we have to offer the world.

How we believe, how we communicate about God, the story you and I have received—it is a prism, a scope, through which the entire world around us makes the most sense. That is what Episcopal means: *Epi* means "on or above," and *scope* means "to see in order to act, to target, to observe." Our unique Episcopal version of the gospel understands that we see and act for the whole world—including the man at the gate.

Sharing a Mission and a Message

Because of our common mission, we are uniquely prepared to be God's people in the world. Now we are responsible for sharing it: the mission and the message. There are people outside our doors, and every congregation and person in the Episcopal Church bears a responsibility that leads us unashamedly, unabashedly into the world to meet them. You may not have gold or silver, but you have what you have received: grace and mercy.

It is true that at the end of my life I want to rest in the bosom of Abraham. That is my desire: at day's end, to be embraced by the God who loves me. What I have learned from studying and praying about this is that I am saved by grace alone, *and* I am expected to arrive at heaven's door side-by-side with the one who right now sits patiently at my gate of comfort. I will only arrive there holding the hand of the man at the gate.

chapter eleven

You Are the Answer to Prayer

Almighty and everlasting God, let your fatherly hand ever be over these your servants; let your Holy Spirit ever be with them; and so lead them in the knowledge and obedience of your Word, that they may serve you in this life, and dwell with you in the life to come; through Jesus Christ our Lord. *Amen.*

> — COLLECT SAID AT THE CONCLUSION OF THE BAPTISMAL RITE, FOLLOWING CONFIRMATION, RECEPTION, OR REAFFIRMATION[40]

Then He said to them, "The harvest truly is great, but the laborers are few; therefore pray the Lord of the harvest to send out laborers into His harvest."

> — LUKE 10:2 (NKJV)

ot all translations of Luke's gospel say "*pray* the Lord of the harvest;" many use the word "ask" instead. I think the New King James Version's use of the word "pray" better captures the meaning. The harvest is bountiful, so pray the Lord of the harvest to send laborers into the field.

These words take me back to the parable of the sower, who sowed with wild abandon, scattering seeds so that the gospel fruit came up all around (Mark 4:3–9). Because of that profligate sower, there is a great harvest and it lies in all kinds of soil. So pray for laborers.

It is wonderful to think about the Episcopal Church at its best in the halls of Congress or in service to a world in crisis. By all means, ponder the unique nature of our faith within the greater body of Christ's church. In all of that, we cannot forget our heritage as Episcopalians: we are a missionary people. As we see in the prayer above, which concludes the baptismal rite, we have been filled with the Holy Spirit so that we can serve God in this life and in the life to come. And serving God means serving God's mission. We are the laborers sent into the harvest.

Many Have Labored Before Us

In Luke's gospel Jesus offers his prayer for laborers to enter the harvest in the midst of commissioning a group of seventy people to their mission of healing, preaching, and announcing the reign of God. It is a great moment of anticipation for these first missionaries, but they must have been humbled by how much work there was to be done. "Jesus, the harvest is great. There is so much to do. We need help." "Pray then, all of you," he must have said.

You and I stand at the end of a long line of people who answered that call, who were the answer to Jesus' prayer. The Episcopal Church itself is one founded by missionary clergy and laity who brought with them the Anglican Church of their homeland. Those sowers, those missionaries, came across the ocean bearing wooden boxes filled with books they would use to prepare sermons and instruct people and share the gospel in a new world. The same box served as a bookshelf in their home; it was their first piece of furniture. And it would also serve as a coffin for their return trip home at the end of a long day's labor in the harvesting fields.

The Episcopal Church that we call our spiritual home is not only the great benefactor of great missionary labor; it has also sent missionaries to work in God's fields. In our most recent book of saints past and more contemporary, called *Holy Women, Holy Men*,[41] we remember these missionaries in our daily prayers throughout the year. In the variety of their stories we see the breadth and depth of the good news of God. We hear of missionaries like Robert Hunt, who was the first chaplain at Jamestown in 1607, and Molly Brant, who witnessed to the faith among the Mohawks. We learn about missionary bishops who served the church in Brazil and Tennessee, China and Japan, the Philippines, Haiti, and the Dominican Republic. We see the desire to share the living gospel in the efforts of people as different as Marianne of Molokaii, who was a leper and missionary in Hawaii at the turn of the twentieth century, and Harriet Bedell, a deaconess and missionary

among the Seminole peoples of Florida who died in
1969. In their lives we see what it means to be a sower
of the seed of the gospel in a variety of places and in all
kinds of soil.

We have been blessed with many sowers, many
saints. For me, four of them are essential for understanding the missionary spirit of our Episcopal Church.

The first is *Jackson Kemper.* He was born December 24,
1789, in Pleasant Valley, New York. He grew up an
Episcopalian in the midst of a great missionary revival.
People were flocking to the West, and our church was
sending missionaries to work across the middle of the
young country. Kemper was ordained a priest in 1814,
and by 1835, he was the first missionary bishop to go
West to support the efforts of these pioneering clergy
and laity.[42]

He established a college in St. Louis, Missouri, for
the purpose of raising up young men for the ministry.
He also founded Nashotah House seminary and Racine
College in Wisconsin. He urged extensive outreach to
Native Americans and commissioned translations of the
Bible and church's liturgies into their languages. With
words like these, he brought missionary zeal and con-
viction that inspired generations:

> How remarkably peculiar, how vastly important is
> the position of our Church! Possessing as we fully
> believe all those characteristics which distinguished
> the primitive fold:—A scriptural Liturgy—evangel-
> ical doctrines—and the apostolic succession—hav-

ing the form of godliness *and* the power thereof—
free from the false and worldly scruples and the
time-serving policy of civil governments—indepen-
dent—respected and influential—in the midst of an
intelligent, enterprising and commercial people.
Brethren!...Are we prepared—are we doing at the
present moment *even one tenth* part of what we are
capable?...

With the talents we possess, (and for which, as good
stewards, we must finally account, at that hour
when no secrets can be hid), with the talents committed to our trust and the privileges we enjoy, cannot our faith, our liberality and our self-denial,
greatly increase? Cannot our supplications be more
fervent, our economy more strict, our love of souls
more ardent? Have we, as individuals, or a Church,
a deep and abiding interest in the success of missions?

Not a brother here would I accuse of indifference or
cowardice. But I would stir up, with God's permission, the pure mind of each one, by way of remem-
brance. It is the spirit of missions I earnestly and
most affectionately advocate.[43]

Many a diocese owes its birth and life to the missionary spirit of Jackson Kemper and the faithful leaders
who left their homes to minister in small, frontier
towns, all in order to ensure that their witness to the
good news of Jesus Christ and the particular Episcopal
way of following him grew in the fertile missionary
fields of the West.

Julia Chester Emery was added to the Episcopal Calendar in 1994, on the eve of my General Ordination Exams in preparation for priesthood. I studied her along with the other additions that year; not surprisingly, it was Emery who stood out for me. In fact, one of my treasured books is *A Century of Endeavor,* Emery's chronicle of the great missionary age that included luminaries like Jackson Kemper.

Emery's father was a sea captain and two of her brothers were priests. One sister provided hospitality for missionaries visiting New York City, while faithfully caring for an infirmed sister. Her sister Mary preceded Julia on the Board of Missions, but Julia Chester Emery was the one who served as the national secretary of the Woman's Auxiliary of the Board of Missions from 1876 to 1916.[44]

She managed to visit every diocese in the United States, and further afield to Japan, inland China, Hong Kong, and the Philippines, as she worked to coordinate and encourage mission. She even served as a delegate to the Pan-Anglican Congress in London.

Emery invented the United Thank Offering—a fund organized by women to support mission, which to this day serves as the solid rock on which many missions stand. Her commitment to mission funding had an impact on almost every diocese in the western United States. I am particularly grateful for her efforts to raise money to pay a number of clergy who journeyed to the first foreign field of the Episcopal Church, the strange new land of Texas.

Julia Chester Emery's commitment to mission inspires me as a bishop, for I know I stand on the shoulders of the missionaries who have come before me. She reminds me that the work of countless unnamed men and women who spread the gospel through the unique witness of the Episcopal Church depended on the support of those whose hearts burned for mission and whose giving undergirded the proclamation of the gospel.

Another of my favorite missionaries is *James Theodore Holly*. He was the first African-American bishop in the Episcopal Church, serving the new Diocese of Haiti, and later the Diocese of the Dominican Republic, as well.[45]

Born in 1829 in Washington, D.C., he was the descendant of freed slaves. His great-great grandfather James Theodore Holly was a Scotsman in Maryland. He was the master of several Holly slaves whom he freed in 1772, including his son and namesake, James Theodore Holly.

Holly grew up in the Roman Catholic faith. He connected with Frederick Douglass and other black abolitionists and became active in the anti-slavery movement. He left his home church over a dispute about ordaining local black clergy and joined the Episcopal Church in 1852.

He was a shoemaker, then a teacher and school principal before his own ordination in the Episcopal Church at age twenty-seven. Holly served as rector at St. Luke's Church in New Haven, Connecticut, and in 1856 he helped to found the Protestant Episcopal Society for Promoting the Extension of the Church among Colored People, a forerunner of the Union of Black Episcopalians. This group challenged the church to take a position against slavery at General Convention.

In 1861 he and his family led a group of African Americans who had chosen to settle in Haiti, the world's first black republic. Several members of his family and many other settlers died in Haiti because of disease and the sheer hardship of the mission, but Holly was nevertheless determined to raise up an Episcopal church in that new country. In July 1863, he organized Holy Trinity Church. He established schools and churches, and he trained young men to be priests. He wrote concerning that time that just "as the last surviving apostle of Jesus was in tribulation . . . on the forlorn isle of Patmos, so, by His Divine Providence, [Christ] had brought this tribulation upon me for a similar end in this isle in the Caribbean sea."[46] He paid the highest price, in order to extend the proclamation of Jesus Christ through the unique and particular worship and mission of the Episcopal Church.

In 1874 he was ordained bishop at Grace Church in New York City by the American Church Missionary Society, an evangelical Episcopal branch of the church. Until his death in 1911, he was loyal and driven in his cause: to free black slaves before emancipation and to bring the gospel message and better life to the people of Haiti.

One more missionary story is worth remembering here. *Lillian Trasher* was on auto-pilot in 1909, engaged to be married and minding her own business. Instead, she fell in love with Jesus Christ's mission when she heard a missionary give a testimony about his work in India. She canceled the wedding, sure that God had called her to serve. She did not know where she was going, so she opened the Bible and read the passage before her. It was Acts 7:34: "I have seen, I have seen the affliction of my people which is in Egypt, and I have heard their groaning and am come down to deliver them. And now come, I will send thee to Egypt." Lillian became one of the great missionaries of charity to the children of Egypt. She arrived at a small village called Asyut near the Nile and was at once called to the bedside of a dying mother. After the mother's death, she took the malnourished child and raised her to health. And so began the orphanage for which she is known and loved.[47]

These are just a few of the men and women who have answered the call to share the gospel with people who had not yet heard the good news. Each chose to make his or her witness through the particular vessel of the Episcopal Church, and we pray for a life that reflects the light of these saints.

Called to be Missionaries

Caring for abandoned and malnourished children was Lillian's mission. What is yours? Just as the named and unnamed missionaries and evangelists of our Episcopal heritage heard a call to serve and proclaim the gospel, you are an answer to someone's prayer. You have your own story to tell, you are walking your unique pilgrimage. In this particular place and time in your life you are an answer to the prayers of Jesus, his disciples, and those seventy who prayed to God, "Send out a laborer to join us, Lord, for the harvest is plentiful."

Most of these saints in our church's past had no idea where their witness would take them. So it is okay that you probably do not know where Jesus is leading as you seek to commit to a rule of life and share the good news of Jesus' reconciling love with the world in word and in action. But trust that he *is* leading you.

You may be saying to yourself, "Okay, I get it! I am an Episcopalian and I am supposed to be a missionary. How exactly am I supposed to manage that?"

Let me be clear: You and I can only do this work together and with God's grace. In fact, the whole work of the Christian community is to transform individual lives like ours, such that we all draw closer to Jesus Christ and come to reorient our lives for God's purposes, through the power of the Spirit. Even as that change is unfolding, we can help our church homes to become missionary outposts from which Episcopalians pursue God's mission. And in time, we can help other pilgrims to find respite and their own calling inside and in partnership with our churches.

One of the brothers of the missionary bishop Lucien Lee Kinsolving was our second bishop in the Episcopal Diocese of Texas. His name was George Herbert Kinsolving. Known as Texas George, he was one of the great missionary bishops of Texas. He was invited to the Virginia Theological Seminary in 1902 to give a talk on mission—it lasted three days. Reflecting on the work of the reformers and their mission, he wrote these words:

> [The reformers], you remember, were delegated to remodel an old system which was then, and had been for many centuries, in existence, but which somehow in the lapse of ages had got strangely out of repair, and sadly needed reconstruction. Numbers of her stones had rolled down from the walls of this Zion, and accumulated masses of debris and rubbish were visible on every hand. All things appeared to be crumbling away into decay and ruin; wild beasts of various descriptions had crept through the breaches into the enclosure, and were trampling underfoot the celestial flowers growing within, and making a fearful havoc with the trees and fruits planted in this garden of His by the hand of the Lord Himself; so that earnest and faithful men found it necessary to replace these stones in their former position, to build up again the towers, to remove the dirt, thoroughly renovate the structure and restore it to its original condition.[48]

You and I are created to be a missionary people, and we are remaking and reshaping and reimagining alongside generations that have come before and those yet to come. Even if it seems like you are one of only a few people committed to mission—even if you are not sure where you fit in this big plan of God's—you are not alone in this work of restoration and remodeling. Many have come before. And you can be part of welcoming others to become laborers, too.

Generous Evangelism

Mission is creative and energetic, adventurous and inspirational, and it is inevitable that we will share the story of what we are doing and the God whom we serve. We don't tell people the good news so they get converted to "our" way of doing things. We don't tell people the good news so they will start coming to church. We share the good news because of how Jesus has affected our lives. We listen and talk and share with others our love of Jesus and his Episcopal Church because grace and mercy are contagious.

This generous spirit spreads when it is rooted in love. I share God's love with you because God's love overflows in my life. I am a better person because I discovered God's love and compassion for me. I am a better person because now I know that my value is not based on the world's calculations but on my relationship with the God who created the world. I can't help but tell all that God has revealed to me and how the Episcopal Church lives out this reality in community and service with others.

Such evangelism is epidemic; that is, it spreads. In his book *The Tipping Point: How Little Things Can Make a Big Difference,* Malcolm Gladwell talks about movements as being more like an epidemic than an economy of scale.[49] It only takes a small group of people to spread a powerful idea—or God's love—throughout a whole population.

Think of the small band of twelve disciples, compared to the whole Roman Empire. Or think about those seventy sent out by Jesus, compared to the whole nation of Israel in their day. You and I received the faith from only a few people in the whole scope of mission within the Episcopal Church; those first few missionaries to this colony brought with them the faith we would inherit.

It only takes a few people, making little changes, to become a mass of people who believe the purpose of the church is the transformation of lives and of the world around us. The gospel of Jesus Christ revealed in the life of the Episcopal Church can spread, and it will happen steadily, organically, and exponentially through what I call *generous evangelism.*[50]

Generous evangelism is when our church, out of the sense of abundant grace, overflows its boundaries out into the world. Generous evangelism listens to others as they tell their pilgrim tales of seeking God in the midst of a wilderness culture. Generous evangelism takes place when people are willing to walk with other persons as they make their journey. Generous evangelism waits to hear about, and then names, Jesus Christ in the lives of the others, revealing the icons and images of God acting in each person's life. Generous evangelism invites people into community. It welcomes them. It helps them to find a language, a particularly Episcopal language for entering the faith conversation. This kind of evangelism willingly embodies the Episcopal way of following Jesus. And generous evangelism is concerned with welcoming people into the family and bringing others into a sacramental life with God through the Episcopal Church.

We must work to keep our focus in church on the main thing; sharing the gospel and living it out in this way is that main thing. We are about the renewing, restarting, renovating work of the gospel. It only takes a few of us to remember and reclaim our legacy. It only takes a few to help others to discover the reconciling love of Jesus Christ, so that still more might come to know God in Jesus Christ as their own Savior and Lord.

Taking the Message on the Road

You are the one this church has been praying for. You may doubt me, and you may doubt the power of the Spirit working through you. But I will tell you that there is no news like gospel news, and you are a bearer of that live-giving word. Most of the news we hear goes in one ear and out the other. Most of the news that is posted on Facebook will be changed seconds later. Gospel news, the transformation of people's lives because of their relationship with Jesus Christ, makes a lasting difference. I know this because it is my experience.

Deep in theological conversation with my best friend one day, I blurted out that I didn't need the Scriptures to tell me about the resurrection. My friend was shocked. I was, too. I love and value the Scriptures, to be sure. But the first Christians did not have a New Testament until the middle of the fourth century, and even then most could not read it or have their own copies. The story resonated because they knew resurrection in their lives. And I know the resurrection is true because I have experienced it in my own life. You and I, we have each had resurrection moments, and thanks to our own personal evangelists, we could understand just what was happening. Those faithful ones bore witness to the reality of Jesus Christ and the Holy Spirit at work in our lives. And because of that change, we were forever changed and forever connected. Gladwell offers another insight on this point; he calls such connection "the stickiness factor."[51] When transformation happens, people don't forget.

The only way the tipping point occurs, the only way transformation ripples out in ever wider circles, the only way the harvest blossoms and bears fruit, is through us living and spreading God's mission in the world. You can have a beautiful church, wonderful music, priests and bishops everywhere, but if we are not sharing stories and helping God to change lives, then we are not doing our gospel work.

And yes, that work is needed. Our gospel message of love and hope, our message about how Jesus loves us, and how the Episcopal Church is a special community where that love is real for all kinds and conditions of people, is a message meant for the world. In fact, it is a message that the world needs to hear. Our mission context is a world divided along lines of culture, politics, sexuality, citizenship, and every other kind of demarcation we can think of. Within this church, all those bodies, with all their different ideas, come to know and love Jesus and come to know and love one another. Our world is hungry and starving for the Word of God proclaimed by our kind of church—the Episcopal Church.

The Episcopal Church must leave the building and take its unique and unabashed message on the road. We must go off our property and into the streets. We must go like the servants in the Bible to gather every kind of person into the banquet hall. We must be a church that meets in libraries and coffee shops during the day, then meets in the pubs and late-night diners until dawn. We have got to be a church packing the gospel to go out into the world and unpacking it for folks who believe the church has nothing to offer because they have been beat up enough by religion.

I can promise you that most faith communities are trying to figure out our baffling contemporary cultural context. The megachurches and the little churches and all the denominations are trying to figure this new world out. The Episcopal Church has a track record. Try spreading the gospel in Haiti in the 1800s. If those missionary saints could do it then, surely we can embrace our new mission contexts today.

We have the perfect front porch from which to launch this renewed missionary effort. We have congregations—our own missionary outposts—throughout the nation. Some are in remote locations; others are in the heart of great cities. They serve as way stations for the pilgrims seeking God in the world. They share the bread of the gospel as manna for the journey. They provide shelter from the storm and refuge for those battered by life. And always, they equip and send out the laborers Jesus prayed for.

It is tempting to explore some other calling, as church. Couldn't we just mind our own business and keep this beautiful church and loving God to ourselves? No, day by day, in our words and in our actions, we must show forth the life and mission of Jesus. And we must show those we meet and those who come to us the unique and wonderful spirituality of our own unique Episcopal expression of Christian faith. People will listen and come because they want to hear and engage around our particular view of the world and God and see what it says to their own lives. If they want to hear about other denominations or other religions, they will study them or try them out. If they come to us, they want to hear the gospel and our particular understanding of it. Be warned: seekers can smell inauthenticity and insincerity a mile away. When they come into our churches they are looking for Episcopalians who will talk with them about Jesus . . . and mean it.

The work isn't just a Sunday thing, and it's not just something that happens inside the church. Jesus didn't tell the seventy, "Wait here and I'll go get the people for you." Jesus didn't say, "Wait here in the barn. I'll bring the harvest to you." The harvest is outside.

If you are going to walk the way of Jesus in the Episcopal Church, know that you walk in the long line of missionary brothers and sisters who have been preparing the world for Jesus. When our Savior prays, "How often have I desired to gather your children together as a hen gathers her brood under her wings" (Matthew 23:37), you and I are spread out as his wings, gathering in all the people of Zion.

The world does not need some old idea of church or some narrative long since forgotten, like the crumbling, pre-Reformation church that Texas George described. The world does not need more religious people content in their pews with their private, polite, personal Jesus. The world needs unabashedly Episcopal lovers of Jesus. The world needs a vital, living missionary organism that is in solidarity with the community in which God has planted it.

Unabashedly Episcopalian

How will we know if we are really living into the best of our Episcopal heritage? How will we know if our mission is working? How will we know we are making progress in God's fields?

We will know because our ministries will transform and renew the world as part of the ongoing restoration begun in Christ's resurrection. Our own lives will be characterized by exceptional stewardship—stewardship of the resources of time and money entrusted to us. Our work will be excellence in mission. We will know we are making progress when evangelism (the proclamation of the good news of salvation and the unique story of Jesus Christ) and caring for others become the hallmarks of the Episcopal Church once again.

Yes, I think we should pay attention to our Average Sunday Attendance. It matters that we welcome more people to be fellow laborers through baptism, confirmation, and reception into the Anglican Communion. It matters that the median age (currently fifty-seven) decrease to reflect our mission context (which is closer to thirty-five). We will know we have turned a corner when our leadership—ordained and lay—is more diverse ethnically and more closely tracks with the communities around us. All this is true.

But I believe in my heart that we will really know that we are making a difference in God's kingdom when we see more people connecting to Jesus Christ through our mission, and see people of every age engaged in serious formation and transformation. We will be able to celebrate when every year, every diocese launches new communities (fellowships, missions, parishes), and we see living and dying as healthy expressions of an entrepreneurial church in active relationship and communication with the world in which we minister. We will know we are making progress when we see congregations everywhere reaching out with renewed and creative commitment to improve the lives of their neighbors—in body, mind, and spirit.

The world needs Episcopalians who love others, care for others, need and welcome others. The world needs people of faith who listen first and speak later, who are willing to come out of their comfortable houses of prayer and hear the cries of God's people on the streets. If we are the answer to Jesus' prayer, then we are also the answer to the prayers of the world: those who come to us and those waiting to be found and heard and held. And Jesus is clear: the only way we will find them is if we walk outside, unabashedly living our faith.

Lift up your eyes and see the world is in need of Jesus and those who love and follow him. As I imagine each of us taking up that call, I can't help but recall the inspiring words of Texas George. He concluded his remarks to those priests-to-be, clergy, and missionaries gathered before him at Virginia Seminary with these words:

> The work may be slow and arduous, but in God's time, in His way, and by His means, victory will crown our efforts in the end. "Come it will, and come it must," ... and oh, what a joy and privilege

to feel that we can, indeed, help in such work . . . and share in the ultimate triumph of His glorious cause. The vision comforted St. John at Patmos, when he saw the Holy City, new Jerusalem, coming down out of Heaven from God, having the glory of God. St. Augustine gazed with rapture upon the same entrancing sight, while the Roman Empire was crumbling to pieces around him; and the Voice of God whispers to our souls, even as we speak, and bids us gaze in faith upon a like vision, and even while we look it may cease to be vision by becoming transformed into a consummate reality.[52]

Endnotes

1. "The General Thanksgiving" from the service of Morning Prayer, *The Book of Common Prayer* (New York: Church Hymnal, 1979), 101.

2. Jon Meacham, *American Gospel* (New York: Random House, 2007), 65.

3. Meacham, *American Gospel*, 230.

4. Meacham, *American Gospel*, 160.

5. Meacham, *American Gospel*, 167.

6. Quoted in Meacham, *American Gospel*, 203.

7. The Episcopal Church includes churches in the following countries: United States of America, Taiwan, Micronesia, Honduras, Ecuador, Colombia, Venezuela, Haiti, the Dominican Republic, the Virgin Islands, Puerto Rico, Convocation of Episcopal Churches in Europe (Austria, Belgium, France, Germany, Italy and Switzerland).

8. BCP (1979), 365.

9. BCP (1979), 301.

10. Christian Smith and Melina Lundquist Denton, *Soul Searching: The Religious and Spiritual Lives of American Teenagers* (New York: Oxford University Press, 2005), 162–163.

11. BCP (1979), 857.

12. BCP (1979), 304–305.

13. R. S. Thomas, "The Kingdom," in *Collected Poems 1945–1990* (London: Phoenix Press, 2002), 233. Used by permission.

14. BCP (1979), 304.

15. Words by Lesbia Scott (b. 1898), in *The Hymnal 1982* (New York: Church Hymnal, 1985), hymn 293.

16. BCP (1979), 304.

17. Stan Cohen and Donald Miller, *The Big Burn: The Northwest's Forest Fire of 1910* (Missoula, Mont.: Pictorial Histories Publishing Co., 1978).

18. Peter Ponzio, "A Man on Fire," unpublished poem. Used with permission.

19. BCP (1979), 304.

20. Jonathan Thompson, "Climber Follows Grandmother's Footsteps," March 21, 2004, www.seclimbers.org.

21. Thompson, "Climber Follows Grandmother's Footsteps."

22. BCP (1979), 304.

23. *The Rule of the Society of Saint John the Evangelist* (Cambridge, Mass.: Cowley Publications, 1997), 44.

24. Karl Rahner, *Encounter with Silence: Scriptural Classics* (South Bend, Ind.: St. Augustine's Press, 1999), 219.

25. Richard Meux Benson, quoted in *The Rule of the Society of Saint John the Evangelist,* 51.

26. BCP (1979), 304.

27. BCP (1979), 816.

28. BCP (1979), 305.

29. John Hines, c. 1980. From personal papers used by author to prepare a lecture given to College of Preachers, Washington, D.C.

30. BCP (1979), 305.

31. N. T. Wright, *Surprised by Hope: Rethinking Heaven, the Resurrection, and the Mission of the Church* (New York: HarperCollins, 2008), 185.

32. W. D. Davies and Dale C. Allison, *The Gospel According to Saint Matthew* (Edinburgh: T&T Clark, 1997), 199.

33. John Chrystostom, *Homilies on Matthew,* homily 69; http://www.ccel.org/ccel/schaff/npnf110.iii.LXVI.html.

34. Adapted from the Iona Community's *A Wee Worship Book* (Chicago: GIA Publications, 1999), 95.

35. BCP (1979), 305.

36. Howell Raines, *Fly Fishing through the Midlife Crisis* (New York: Anchor Books, 1994).

37. Quoted in "Sharing the Gospel of Salvation: GS Misc 956" (London: General Synod of the Church of England, 2010), sec. 72.

38. "Sharing the Gospel of Salvation," sec. 73.

39. "Sharing the Gospel of Salvation," sec. 11.

40. BCP (1979), 310.

41. *Holy Women, Holy Men: Celebrating the Saints* (New York: Church Publishing Inc., 2010).

42. "Jackson Kemper," *Holy Women, Holy Men,* 384.

43. Jackson Kemper, "The Duty of the Church with Respect to Missions," a sermon preached before the Board of Missions of the Protestant Episcopal Church in the United States, in St. Paul's Chapel, New York, October 7, 1841.

44. "Julia Chester Emery," *Holy Women, Holy Men,* 162.

45. "James Theodore Holly," *Holy Women, Holy Men,* 270.

46. Quoted in "James Theodore Holly," *Holy Women, Holy Men,* 270.

47. "Lillian Trasher," *Holy Women, Holy Men,* 126.

48. George Herbert Kinsolving, "The Church's Burden" (New York: Edwin S. Gorham, 1902), chap. 1; http://anglicanhistory.org/usa/ghkinsolving/burden1902/01.html.

49. Malcolm Gladwell, *The Tipping Point: How Little Things Can Make a Big Difference* (New York: Back Bay Books, 2002) 2.

50. For more on "generous evangelism," see the author's series of evangelism lectures given in November 2011, www.adoyle.libsyn.com/webpage/2011/11.

51. Gladwell, *The Tipping Point*, 19.

52. Kinsolving, "The Church's Burden," chap. 3; http://anglicanhistory.org/usa/ghkinsolving/burden1902/03.html.